The Fool's Journey

The Sacred Circle Tarot is rich with possibilities for personal growth. Each card is embedded with multi-leveled symbolic triggers for meditation. As you reflect upon the Major Arcana cards, you undertake "The Journey of The Fool"—a mystical trek that parallels your personal life journey and the evolution of spirit toward initiation.

To clarify the stages of this spiritual journey and to evoke the Pagan nature of this deck, *The Sacred Circle Tarot* modifies the traditional names and sequential order of the Major Arcana cards. Thus, the zero card depicts The Green Man, who symbolizes primal energy. The Green Man triggers your evolution, propelling you through an unfolding spiral of experience, knowledge, and wisdom.

Taken in order from zero to twenty-one, the *The Sacred Circle Tarot* cards lead you from the first awakening of consciousness to dissolution of your old self, initiation, rebirth, and enlightenment. As patterns and lessons emerge, you will start to understand where your life path is taking you.

The fool's journey ends, but yours is only beginning.

About the Creators of
The Sacred Circle Tarot

The Artist

Paul Mason was born in Leicester, England, in 1951. He studied fine art in college and, since graduating, has worked as a graphic designer, photographer, and illustrator in both paper-based and electronic interactive media. He has had several exhibitions of landscape photography and his photographs have appeared on postcards and greeting cards, as well as in the photographic press. Paul has illustrated two books, *Herb Craft* and *Familiars: The Animal Powers of Britain*, as well as designing and illustrating book covers. In the past, he has taught photography and communication skills and was employed as a designer and illustrator by zoos and conservation organizations. At present, he designs interactive multimedia for De Montfort University, U. K.

The Author

Anna Franklin was born some years ago (though not as many as Paul) in the English Midlands. After gaining an honors degree in fine art photography, she worked for some years as a lecturer in fine art and media studies, and as a photographer and illustrator. Increasingly, she found that her work as a Priestess of the native British Pagan Tradition took more and more of her time, and decided to retrain as a therapist in reflexology, massage, and aromatherapy to augment the traditional craft skills of herbalism and counseling. She has run a number of courses in personal and spiritual development, healing, and magic, and has written several books on Pagan subjects including *Herb Craft* (with Sue Lavender); *Familiars: The Animal Powers of Britain*; *Pagan Feasts* (with Sue Phillips); and *Personal Power*. She is the editor of the long-standing British Pagan magazine *Silver Wheel* and co-editor of the fantasy magazine *Strix*.

the
Sacred
Circle
tarot

a celtic pagan journey

Written by
Anna Franklin

Illustrated by
Paul Mason

Llewellyn Publications
Woodbury, Minnesota

FIRST EDITION

Tenth Printing, 2008

Cover design by Lynne Menturweck
Book editing and design by Astrid Sandell

Library of Congress Cataloging-in-Publication Data
Franklin, Anna.
    The sacred circle tarot : a Celtic pagan journey / Anna Franklin ; illustrated by Paul Mason. — 1st ed.
        p.   cm.
    ISBN 13: 978-1-56718-457-0
    ISBN 10: 1-56718-457-X (trade paper)
    1. Tarot. 2. Mythology, Celtic—Miscellanea. 3. Goddess religion—British Isles—Miscellanea.   I. Title.
    BF1879.T2F72   1998
    133.3'2424—dc21   98-12667
                                                          CIP

Llewellyn Publications
A Division of Llewellyn Worldwide, Ltd.
2143 Wooddale Drive, Dept. 978-1-56718-457-0
Woodbury, MN 55125-2989
http://www.llewellyn.com
Llewellyn is a registered trademark of Llewellyn Worldwide, Ltd.
Printed in the United States of America
Cards printed in Belgium

Dedication

*For our partners Enda Mason
and John White in gratitude
for their love and support.*

To Write to the Creators

If you wish to contact the author or artist, or would like more information about this book, please write to the author in care of Llewellyn Worldwide and we will forward your request. Both the author and the publisher appreciate hearing from you and learning of your enjoyment of this book and how it has helped you. Llewellyn Worldwide cannot guarantee that every letter written to the author or artist can be answered, but all will be forwarded. Please write to:

Anna Franklin or Paul Mason
c/o Llewellyn Worldwide
2143 Wooddale Drive, Dept. 978-1-56718-457-0
Woodbury, MN 55125-2989, U.S.A.

Please enclose a self-addressed envelope and international reply coupon for reply.

Contents

Minor Arcana: Swords, Wands, Cups, and Discs

Preface

The Development of *The Sacred Circle Tarot*

A few years ago—well, let's be honest, quite a few years ago—Paul Mason and I attended the same art college in Coventry, in the English Midlands. Shortly after we had completed our degrees, we made our first attempt at designing a tarot. This was to be a very different deck, based on collages of photographic images. However, lack of money and the sheer scale of the undertaking defeated us, and the project was shelved for fifteen years. Then Paul discovered that he could seamlessly combine photographic images on a computer and resurrected the idea. I set to work, taking some of the photographs later used in the deck and drafting a series of concepts. Paul took a lot more photographs and skillfully executed my original ideas, combining our photographs and his own drawings to create stunning images in a way that is beyond me—though we did have a few run-ins when I wanted a particular symbol included and Paul thought another would look prettier! After two years we finally had a series of pictures we were both happy with—and we even managed to include some of our original photographs.

—Anna Franklin

The Development of the Images

Anna and I first started work on this project over fifteen years ago. Our ambition was to produce a tarot that was rich in the Pagan and mythological iconography of the British Isles and Ireland, using photography to give a level of naturalism and sense of place that we felt was lacking in other cards. Although some of these images were successful, the difficulties of combining them into a coherent whole using traditional photographic techniques proved impractical. The project lay dormant for a number of years until computer image manipulation programs came along. Some of these earlier pictures appear in *The Sacred Circle Tarot*; Anna's and my younger selves are featured as the Queen of Swords and Page of Swords, respectively. In the course of other work, I became aware of the possibilities of continuing with this project using Adobe Photoshop, a highly sophisticated computer graphics program.

The tarot was produced using a combination of photographs (scanned into the Kodak PhotoCD format), pencil drawings colorized and enhanced by computer, and elements drawn and constructed directly in computer graphics applications. This combination of media was then assembled in Photoshop and the color, contrast, and density of each element adjusted to produce a more harmonious whole. When the composition was completed, I applied a filter to give a more painterly appearance, varying the degree of effect to different parts of the picture. At this stage, I also applied lighting effects, such as stars and rays of light. The final aim was to produce a tarot that had some of the naturalism of photography, but also had a magical realism that did justice to the subject.

—Paul Mason

An Introduction

The Sacred Circle Tarot

The British Pagan Tradition

There are many paths we can follow in mundane life, just as there are many religious paths we can follow in our spiritual lives. As Pagans we believe that all religious paths (whether Muslim, Hindu, Jewish, Christian, and so forth) ultimately lead back to the same source, the Divine Spirit. The ways we perceive the Divine Spirit, and the names we give to it, are the result of cultural differences, and therefore we all take different routes in our spiritual quest. However, we believe that this quest is for the individual, and each person must find his or her own path.

Pagans have a particularly diverse number of sects. There are as many ways to approach Paganism as there are people within it. Finding your own true path involves a long search within yourself and without. Groups will pass on their own particular teachings and viewpoints; these may coincide with how you think and would like to work, they may not. This is not to say that one way is more valid than another. You have to find the way that is true for you. Paganism is a religious impulse rather than a religious dogma.

This deck is based on the teachings of the British Pagan Tradition. Central to our path is a relationship with the land in a real, not symbolic, manner. We observe and celebrate the wheel of the seasons and become part of their ebb and flow. The spirits of the land—the Gods and Goddesses, the Wildfolk, the animals and plants—are sought and honored for their teachings.

The influences on British Paganism have been many and varied, each has been absorbed within the consciousness of the population and the land itself.

The great megalithic temples, standing stones, and burial chambers of Britain and Ireland were constructed in the Neolithic period by the aboriginal people of Britain. They were concerned with the Cult of the Dead, recognizing the condition of humankind reflected in the death and regeneration of the passing seasons, the monthly waxing and waning of the moon, and the yearly weakening and strengthening of the sun in its cycles. During the Bronze Age (2200–1000 B.C.E.), the introduction of metals saw great changes in the structure of society, with more emphasis on personal wealth and a move away from the building of megaliths to water cults.

The first Goidelic (Gaelic-speaking Irish, Scots, Manx) Celts arrived in Britain around 900 B.C.E. Some time between 500 and 250 B.C.E., the Brythonic or British-speaking Celts (Welsh, Cornish, and Breton) arrived. It is thought that the Celts absorbed many of the indigenous beliefs and that the Druids made use of astronomical temples, such as Stonehenge. The influence of the Druids and the celebration of the great festivals has left an indelible legacy that can be discerned in lore and folk practices up to the present day.

The Roman invasion of England and Wales was completed around 100 C.E. and lasted until 500 C.E. (Ireland was not occupied by Rome and remained largely unaffected). One of the reasons for the success of the Roman Empire was that they did not impose their own religion on their subject nations, but fostered a fusion between local deities and their own gods; Celtic gods were worshiped alongside Roman deities. The Celtic religion was affected by Roman culture to varying degrees in different parts of the country.

The Heathen Saxons began to invade after the withdrawal of the Romans and settled around 450 C.E., the Danes around 800 C.E. The real Christianization of Britain began in 597 C.E. with missionaries led by St. Augustine. The Germanic rulers were converted, and within a hundred years the population was nominally Christian. However, the rural population was still largely Celtic and apparently clung to the old religion, accepting the changes in name only. The old festivals were still celebrated, but had different names. The old places of worship were often overbuilt with churches and remained sacred; the old sacred wells and their presiding spirits were called holy wells, and the spirits sometimes became Christian saints (like the goddess Brighid). The Viking invasion in the ninth century led to a revival of Paganism, demonstrating perhaps that the populace was not as much converted to Christianity as the church would have liked to believe.

The modern British Pagan has inherited the legacy of all these disparate influences, tempered by the spirit of the land itself. We seek not to impose concepts within our worship, but to understand what the earth has to teach us, to live with the earth, not to impose our will upon it.

The "world-view" of the Pagan is essentially different from the normally accepted materialistic view of Western Society. To the Pagan, everything possesses spirit, a living force within it that vibrates to the pulse of the earth itself. It is the Divine energy of the Goddess and the God that permeates everything—people, animals, plants, rocks, the land itself. This energy forms a web of being, a net of power that links and gives life to the cosmos: a concept recognized by witches and shamans worldwide. In Saxon countries it was called "The Web of Wyrd" (*wyrd* roughly means *fate*). The shamanic view of the world is that everything is connected. Any vibration on the web eventually reverberates everywhere else, like ripples moving out from a stone thrown into a pond. As our understanding and consciousness grows, we become aware of the working of the web and its more subtle realms. We are part of the web, can attune to its various energies and magically vibrate the web with full knowledge of the outcome. The magician can integrate and communicate with the web, and through its fibers, perform magic. The Pagan recognizes and works with this force, knowing that because this force is Divine, all things that contain it are sacred. Manifest Nature is sacred.

We celebrate eight great festivals a year—the winter and summer solstices, the spring and autumn equinoxes, and the four fire festivals of our Celtic ancestors (Samhain, Imbolc, Beltane, and Lughnasa). These festivals teach us about the ebb and flow of the year, about life, growth, death, and renewal. In addition, we recognize the monthly waxing and waning of the moon, the increase and decrease of energies. Taken together, these teach us about the relevance of both masculine and feminine forces, the God and the Goddess. Woven within the fabric of these seasonal changes are the life cycles of animals and plants that have important practical and magical lessons. Our framework of operating is a symbolic key to other levels of being. This key evolves with each turning of the cycle.

The primary business of the magician is the transformation of the magician himself. Magic is a constantly expanding state of consciousness, an awareness of the subtle workings of the universe. In the Craft our awareness begins with the cycles of manifest Nature and the creative forces behind them. The Wheel of the Year is our magical paradigm. By working with it and in it, year after year, we can undergo a spiral of expanding consciousness. Our highest aim is to draw down that consciousness into the manifest world.

The Sacred Circle Tarot

The Sacred Circle Tarot is a seventy-eight card deck drawing on the Pagan heritage of Britain and Ireland, its sacred sites, and symbolic imagery from the tradition. We have tried to make this a truly Pagan deck and remove some of the Cabalistic and Christian iconography that has crept into the tarot over the centuries.

Themed tarot decks are very popular and a number have appeared in recent years that use imagery from different traditions (Nordic, Celtic, Greek mythology, etc.). However, it was our aim to formulate a deck that not only draws on ancient traditions but is of immediate relevance to the modern-day practitioner. We felt that the deck should not only be beautiful, but useful; not only useful, but beautiful, using key symbols to unlock the deepest levels of Pagan teaching.

R. J. Stewart suggests that the tarot had its origins in "the story telling traditions and images preserved by travelling entertainers, originally the bards or *filid* of Celtic culture." He points out that the images of the tarot have clear connections with images described in the *Vita Merlini*, a text that pre-dates the earliest known tarot deck by three centuries. It clearly describes the Empress, the Hanged Man, The Wheel of Fortune, The Fool, and so on, which are derived from the bardic Celtic tradition of preserving images of the gods, goddesses, and cosmology. Death appears as the Celtic Death

Goddess and the Devil as the Underworld aspect of the God. This derivation of the tarot from bardic tradition is also clearly seen in the four suits, which represent the four magical weapons of the four directions of the Tuatha De Danaan: the sword of Nuadha (associated with the east); the spear of Lugh (associated with the south), which became wands or rods; the cauldron of the Dagda (associated with the west), which became the cups; and the stone of Fal, which became discs and later pentacles.

We have tried to restore the Celtic Pagan imagery in a way that speaks to, and is of use to, modern Pagans. The imagery of the card is designed to work on a number of levels and to be used not only for divination, but to facilitate personal and spiritual development and to aid in meditation.

The circle of the title is not only the Wheel of the Year, but the sacred circles of the landscapes and the cycles of life—spiritual, material, and emotional.

The cards depict landscapes and sacred sites in Britain and Ireland, centers of energy and worship for thousands of years, emphasizing our connection to the land and its cycles and the visible and spiritual legacy of our ancestors.

In the native magical tradition, each plant and animal has a place (or places) on the wheel, a magical connection within the web of being, and a spiritual lesson. These feature strongly in the imagery of the deck, as do archetypes of Gods and Goddesses.

The Major Arcana

The Major Arcana consists of the normal twenty-two cards, though in some cases the titles and sequence have been altered to fit more closely with the theme of the deck: 0—The Green Man (Fool); 1—The High Priest (Magician); 2—The High Priestess; 3—The Lady (Empress); 4—The Lord (Emperor); 5—The Druid (Heirophant); 6—The Lovers; 7—The Chariot; 8—The Warrior (Strength); 9—The Shaman (Hermit); 10—The Wheel; 11—The Web (Justice); 12—Sacrifice (the Hanged Man); 13—Death; 14—The Underworld (The Devil); 15—The Tower; 16—Initiation

(Temperance); 17—The Star; 18—The Moon; 19—The Sun; 20—Rebirth (Judgement); and 21—The World Tree (The World).

Each of the cards has a divinatory meaning concerned with the currents, energies, and events surrounding the querent. The text explains the relevant symbolism and lessons of various elements of the cards—plants, animals, deities, sacred sites, and so on. These can be used to work on personal and spiritual development independently of the pack. The cards have lessons to teach about self-development, self-improvement, and the healing of the mind and spirit.

On a spiritual level, through the Journey of the Fool, the cards chart the progress of the initiate from undirected energy, through the lessons of dawning consciousness, the death and dissolution of the old self, renewal, and the emergence of the new Self and new consciousness.

The Minor Arcana

The Minor Arcana consists of the usual four suits—cups, wands, discs, and swords—with the cards one to ten and page, knight, queen, and king. They are numbered below and have a key word above, which explains the basic energy of the card.

The minor arcana cards further explore the theme of the Wheel of the Year with each suit corresponding to a different season. They expound on the themes of the Major Arcana and the balancing of the elements and their qualities within the Self. Each suit has its own lessons: swords on the development of mental abilities and the gathering of knowledge; wands on the spiritual and creative impulse; cups on the emotions and spiritual growth; discs on the material plane and the practical application of what has been learned.

The King of each suit, instead of having a key word, is assigned one of the elements and represents the quintessence of that element, while the Ace represents its basic impulse. The Queens represent its mutable qualities; the knights, its fixed qualities; and the pages, its cardinal qualities.

Swords

The suit of swords is associated with the season of spring, the athame of the magician, the direction of the east, sunrise, the element of air, and the power of the mind. The lessons and key words of the suit of swords are all concerned with mental qualities and attributes, how they are used and how they can be developed.

The border of the sword suit consists of skyscapes and clouds with yellow cornerstones, the magical color correspondence of the element of air.

Wands

The suit of wands is associated with the season of summer; the wand, arrow, or spear; the direction of the south; noonday; the element of fire; the power of transmutation; the spiritual impulse; and the energy of creativity. The lessons and key words of this suit are concerned with creativity and energy, how to develop these qualities and crystallize them into practical applications.

The border of the wand suit consists of flames. The cornerstones are red, the magical color correspondence of the element of fire.

Cups

The suit of cups is associated with the season of autumn; the cup, grail, or cauldron; the direction of the west; twilight; the element of water; the emotions; intuition; psychic faculties; and the growth of the spirit. The lessons and key words of this suit are concerned with balancing the emotions and nurturing the spirit.

The border of the cup suit consists of flowing water with blue cornerstones, the magical color correspondence of the element of water.

Discs

The suit of discs is associated with the season of winter; the disc, shield, or stone; the direction of the north; midnight; the element of earth; practical and material matters. The key words and lessons of this suit are mainly concerned with the material plane, the body, and physical health.

The border of the disc suit represents earth and stone. The cornerstones are green, the magical color correspondence of the element of earth.

The Journey of the Fool

Experienced tarot readers might note that I have slightly changed the order of some of the Major Arcana cards. I have done this to clarify the Journey of the Fool, which is one of the titles sometimes given to the Major Arcana. Taken in order from zero to twenty-two, the cards describe a spiritual journey from the first awakening of consciousness to initiation and enlightenment.

Thus, I begin with the Green Man as primal energy, and go on to pair the High Priest and the High Priestess—rather than the Magician and the High Priestess—as encounters with the male and female sides of the Self. The divinatory meanings of the High Priest remain similar to those of the traditional Magician. The candidate then encounters the Goddess and the God within nature, as the Lady and the Lord.

The card normally called the Hierophant or Pope (in some more modern decks, The High Priest) I have called The Druid, the chief priest of the Celts, whose role was similar to that of a hierophant. It took many years of training to become a druid and I have used the image to portray a person who has learned to balance the forces of the preceding cards—raw energy, the male and female sides of himself, and the knowledge of the God and Goddess within nature.

Then follow the lessons of life in the cards of The Lovers, The Chariot, The Warrior (Strength), and the turning toward the lessons of spirit in The Shaman (The Hermit).

Next comes the awareness of the turning of the Wheel (The Wheel of Fortune) and the awareness that everything that moves within the Wheel is connected by The Web (Justice) and that actions have consequences. With this profound realization comes the descent into initiation; first one must be willing to sacrifice the ego and little Self (Sacrifice/The Hanged Man), the old self then dies (Death) and passes to the Underworld (The Devil), where the spirit is tested and refined.

The final dissolution of the old Self (which is described in shamanic initiation experiences as dismemberment and reduction to the bone-seed) is completed with the Tower, where the man-made structure of deceptive self-image and barriers is finally destroyed, allowing the candidate to go forward to Initiation (Temperance). I think that the significance of the Temperance card is often underplayed in tarot interpretations; Crowley changed its name to "Art," and when looked at this way it is one of the most powerful cards in the deck.

Then follows the emergence from initiation in the conventional order of The Star, The Moon, The Sun, Rebirth (Judgement), and The World Tree (The World).

The Journey of the Fool is further described within the body of this text, and its application is explored in the section on using the cards for meditation and spiritual development, beginning on page 24.

Reading the Tarot—Divination

The Zodiac Spread

In this spread, twelve cards are laid out in a circle (figure 1, page 12). Each position corresponds to one of the twelve houses of the zodiac, beginning with Aries (position one) and ending with Pisces (position twelve). This layout tells you about current trends in all areas of your life that will shape your near future and continue to have resonances in the more distant future. It will point out problem areas where you may wish to make changes.

To begin your reading, shuffle the tarot deck thoroughly, taking care to invert some of the cards so that some of the reverse meanings may be used. As you shuffle the cards, think about the question you want the tarot to answer. Next, lay out the first twelve

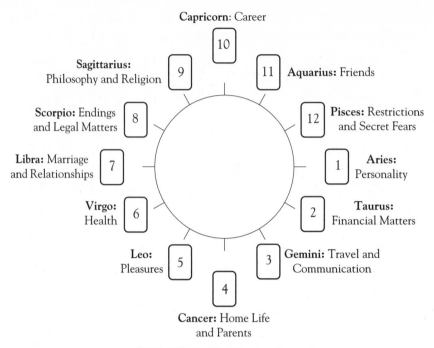

FIGURE 1. *The Zodiac Spread.*

cards from the top of the pack, beginning at position one. Then, once all cards have been laid out, begin your reading with the card in position one.

Card One: *Aries: Personality.* This card will give general clues to the personality of the querent (the person for whom the reading is being made; this might be yourself). This innate personality will affect and color the querent's attitude toward all areas of their life.

Card Two: *Taurus: Financial Matters.* This card is concerned with the material circumstances of the querent—financial position and so on. The indications of this card can be cross-referenced with card eight (legal matters) and card ten (career).

Card Three: *Gemini: Travel and Communication.* This card will indicate any travel opportunities that might arise out of present circumstances, and moreover any news, letters, or other kinds of communication that the querent can expect to receive that will prove to be important.

Card Four: *Cancer: Home Life and Parents*. This card is concerned with the background of the querent, their upbringing and relationship with their parents, or the circumstances of their present home life.

Card Five: *Leo: Pleasures*. This card indicates the things that give the querent pleasure, perhaps their hobbies or interests and the areas from which the querent can derive stimulation and satisfaction.

Card Six: *Virgo: Health*. Card six will show the state of the querent's health or circumstances that might affect their health—physical, emotional, or spiritual—such as environmental factors, stress, or worries.

Card Seven: *Libra: Marriage and Relationships*. This card concerns the closest current relationships of the querent or relationships that will be brought about by present events and trends.

Card Eight: *Scorpio: Endings and Legal Matters*. This card will indicate matters that are coming to a logical conclusion—this might be a relationship, residence in a certain town or dwelling, a job, or a course of study. Such endings may be perceived as negative or positive. Card eight is also concerned with any legal matters that the querent may be involved in at the present time or in the near future as a result of present events.

Card Nine: *Sagittarius: Philosophy and Religion*. This card is concerned with the querent's personal view of spirituality and may offer some advice on the path to follow or how they may develop themselves in these areas. This card can be cross-referenced with cards one (personality) and twelve (fears and restrictions).

Card Ten: *Capricorn: Career*. This card will show current trends or interests in the querent's career. It may offer advice on areas that can be developed into a future career.

Card Eleven: *Aquarius: Friends.* Card eleven will show the querent's attitude toward their friends and how their friends perceive them.

Card Twelve: *Pisces: Restrictions and Secret Fears.* This card gives insight into the things that hold back the querent and prevent him or her from achieving all that they might. It may show areas that need to be explored, worked through, and healed before the querent can go forward.

The Circle Spread

In this spread (figure 2, page 15), nine cards are laid out in a circle, which represents the Wheel of the Year and the elemental correspondences. One card is laid in the center of the circle to represent the querent and the other eight cards represent the querent's strengths and weaknesses and areas the querent needs to work on. This layout is concerned with the inner, spiritual aspects of the querent's life and may offer advice on how to progress.

To begin your reading, shuffle the tarot deck thoroughly, taking care to invert some of the cards so that some of the reverse meanings may be used. As you shuffle the cards, think about the question you want the tarot to answer. Next, lay out the first nine cards from the top of the pack, beginning at position one. Once all cards have been laid out, begin your reading with the card in position one. All cards in this spread relate to the present time.

Card One: *The Querent.* This card corresponds to the center of the circle, where all times and places are one and are connected to all other realms. The querent stands at the center of the circle and has access to all the realms and may choose or reject what is offered to him or her, negative or positive. This card indicates the present circumstances of the querent in his or her personal quest for knowledge.

Card Two: *Mental Aspects.* This card corresponds to the direction of the east, the element of air, the sword, the season of spring,

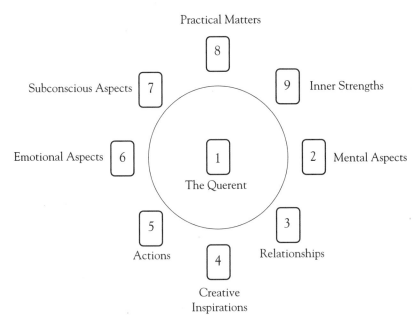

FIGURE 2. *The Circle Spread.*

and the dawn (i.e., beginnings). Its station on the wheel is the spring equinox, which we call Ostara, when new life germinates and emerges with the increase of life and warmth. Magically, air rules all mental activity, from the inception of an idea to abstract knowledge, to the questioning of established theories. Air is the inspiration of life-giving breath, the gentle breeze on the plain, the rushing wind on the mountain top and the destructive hurricane. It is the power of sound, the vocalization of ideas, and the communication of knowledge. This is the place where the querent develops mental powers— ideas, imagination, where questions are asked and knowledge is received. This card will indicate what the querent should work on to balance this area of life.

Card Three: *Relationships.* This card is placed on the southeast point of the circle and corresponds to the start of summer and the festival of Beltane (which means "bright-fire"), a May celebration of life and fertility. The weather is getting warmer, the seeds have been planted and the young animals have been born. We rejoice in the change of weather and energy. At Beltane the Lord and Lady approach their sacred marriage, which gives life to the earth. It is the time of the union of opposites to make a single whole that is greater than the sum of its parts. This card is concerned with relationships, lovers, and close friendships that will either help you grow or prevent progress.

Card Four: *Creative Inspirations.* This card corresponds to the direction of the south and the element of fire, the wand, the season of summer, and noonday. Its station on the wheel is the midsummer solstice, which we call Coamhain, when the earth flowers and grows lush in the heat. Magically, fire rules creativity, life energy, and the spirit. Fire is the illumination within, the force of the spirit. It is the glow of the candle flame, the warmth of the hearth, the burning heat of the desert, and the incandescence of the sun—the fire that both purifies and destroys. Fire is the power of inner sight and creative vision, directing it and controlling it to make it manifest in the world. This card will indicate what the querent should work on to balance this area of life.

Card Five: *Actions.* This card corresponds to the direction of southwest and the festival of Lughnasa, the high summer celebration of the ripening corn and the start of the harvest. The ancients celebrated the occasion with gatherings, games, and contests. This card gives advice on positive actions that you need to take at this point in your development and is also concerned with the development of your masculine side.

Card Six: *Emotional Aspects.* This card corresponds to the direction of the west, the element of water, the cup or cauldron, and the season of autumn. Its station on the wheel is Herfest, the autumn equinox, which marks the harvest and the completion of the vegetation cycle of the year, as the days begin to grow colder and the light declines. It is the time of fullness and maturity. Magically, water rules emotions and feelings, including love and hate, daring and cowardice, happiness and sorrow, giving and taking. It also rules the intuition and psychic skills. Water is cleansing and purifying. It is the power of experience. Water can be the safety of the uterine waters of the womb, the cleansing stream, the deep pool of the subconscious mind, the nourishing river, the brew of initiation, the movement of the tides, and the power of the sea to give bounty or destroy with its tempest. This card will indicate what the querent should work on to balance the emotional area of their life.

Card Seven: *Subconscious Aspects.* This card corresponds to the northwest and the festival of Samhain, the start of winter. Samhain is the hinge of the year, when one year turns to the next. It is a potent time between times, when the veils between the worlds are thin and the Otherworld is very close. The energies of Samhain relate to deep inner journeys and this card advises you on the subconscious or deeply rooted base of the Inner Self, which will either block or aid your progress and may offer advice on how to begin dealing with it.

Card Eight: *Practical Matters.* This card corresponds to the direction of the north; the element of earth; the pentacle, shield or stone; the season of winter; and midnight. Its station on the wheel is the midwinter solstice, which we call Yule, when the sun is reborn at the dead time of the year when the earth sleeps. From this point on, the days begin to lengthen once more and though the worst of the winter weather is still to come, we have the promise of the return of spring. Magically, the earth rules the body and the material plane, including such things as money and possessions. Earth is solid, the manifest world that supports and nourishes us. It is the standing stone beneath the stars, the silent cave, the sacred grove, the high mountain peak, the fertile fields, the crystals, rocks and stones—our home planet. It is the power of touch and all that is solid and tangible. This is the place where the querent develops his or her practical powers of manifestation. This card will indicate what the querent should work on to balance this area of their life.

Card Nine: *Inner Strengths.* This card corresponds to the Northeast and the festival of Imbolc, when the light is noticeably return-ing after the winter dark. New shoots are visible on the bare earth and give us the promise of spring, the return of greenery and life and warmth. This card indicates what the querent's inner strengths are to draw upon and build on. It also relates to the development of their feminine, intuitive, nurturing side.

Planetary Spread

This spread, relating to the present time and near future, uses seven cards laid out in a seven-pointed star under the auspices of the seven planets known to the ancients and their influences (figure 3, below).

To begin your reading, shuffle the tarot deck thoroughly, taking care to invert some of the cards so that some of the reverse meanings may be used. As you shuffle the cards, think about the question you want the tarot to answer. Next, lay out the first seven cards from the top of the pack, beginning at position one. Then, once all cards have been laid out, begin your reading with the card in position one.

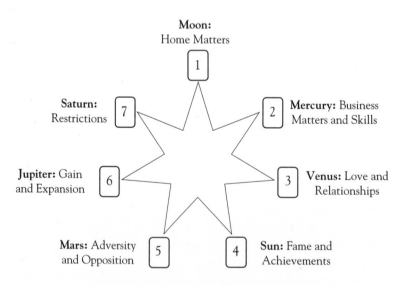

FIGURE 3. *The Planetary Spread.*

Card One: *Moon.* Home matters.

Card Two: *Mercury.* Business matters and skills.

Card Three: *Venus.* Love and relationships.

Card Four: *Sun.* Fame and achievements.

Card Five: *Mars.* Adversity and opposition.

Card Six: *Jupiter.* Gain and expansion.

Card Seven: *Saturn.* Restrictions.

The Romany Spread

This spread uses twenty-one cards and gives a detailed reading of past, present, and future trends (figure 4, page 20). Three rows of seven cards are laid out, which may be read both horizontally and vertically, following the topics presented in the spread diagram. For example, card four relates to financial matters in the past, card eleven to present finances, and card eighteen to future financial circumstances.

To begin your reading, shuffle the tarot deck thoroughly, taking care to invert some of the cards so that some of the reverse meanings may be used. As you shuffle the cards, think about the question you want the tarot to answer. Next, lay out the first twenty-one cards from the top of the pack, beginning at position one. Then, once all cards have been laid out, begin your reading with the card in position one.

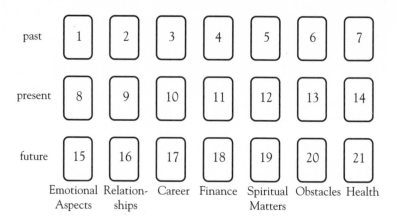

past   1   2   3   4   5   6   7

present   8   9   10   11   12   13   14

future   15   16   17   18   19   20   21

Emotional Relation- Career Finance Spiritual Obstacles Health
Aspects   ships   Matters

FIGURE 4. *The Romany Spread.*

The Web Spread

The Web Spread uses seventeen cards to investigate past, present, and future trends (figure 5, page 21). It demonstrates how one area of life affects another, as each element can be connected on the web. For example, card one relates to the querent, card two to their present circumstances, and card twelve to actions called for. Read across the grid the other way, card three is present relationships and card thirteen future relationships. Card thirteen is further linked to card sixteen (emotional aspects) and card fifteen (obstacles). The linkages of this spread can be read to determine which actions and influences affect particular areas of the querent's life.

To begin your reading, shuffle the tarot deck thoroughly, taking care to invert some of the cards so that some of the reverse meanings may be used. As you shuffle the cards, think about the question you want the tarot to answer. Next, lay out the first seventeen cards from the top of the pack, beginning at position one. Then, once all cards have been laid out, begin your reading with the card in position one.

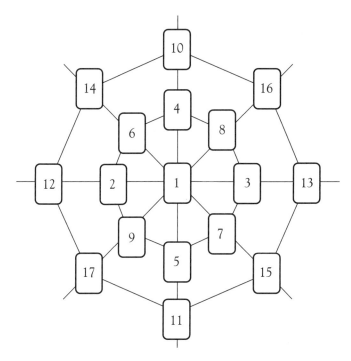

FIGURE 5. *The Web Spread.*

Card One: *The Querent.* This card represents the person for whom the reading is being made.

Card Two: *Present Circumstances of the Querent.*

Card Three: *Present Relationships.*

Card Four: *Present Trends.* This card indicates the influences and energies that most closely surround the querent at the present time.

Card Five: *Present Financial Situation.*

Card Six: *Past Circumstances.* This card shows the past events and circumstances that have shaped the present life of the querent.

Card Seven: *Karmic Consequences.* This card demonstrates the consequences of past actions of the querent, whether for good or ill.

Card Eight: *Past Relationships.*

Card Nine: *Creative Inspirations.* This card indicates what will inspire the querent and where he or she should look for such inspiration.

Card Ten: *Future Circumstances.*

Card Eleven: *Future Financial Situation.*

Card Twelve: *Actions Called For in the Present.*

Card Thirteen: *Future Relationships.*

Card Fourteen: *Subconscious Restrictions.*

Card Fifteen: *Obstacles.* What factors are preventing the querent from progressing.

Card Sixteen: *Emotional Aspects.*

Card Seventeen: *Career.*

The Celtic Cross Spread

This spread uses ten cards and investigates past and present trends and the future outcome (figure 6, page 23).

To begin your reading, shuffle the tarot deck thoroughly, taking care to invert some of the cards so that some of the reverse meanings may be used. As you shuffle the cards think about the question you want the tarot to answer. Next, lay out the first ten cards from the top of the pack, beginning at position one. Then, once all cards have been laid out, begin your reading with the card in position one.

Card One: *The Querent.* This card represents the personality of the querent.

Card Two: *Present Obstacles.* This card represents those obstacles or influences that stand in the way of the querent.

Card Three: *Present Situation.* This card represents the influences that most closely surround the querent at the present time and the situation that they find themselves in.

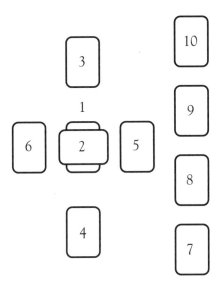

FIGURE 6. *The Celtic Cross Spread.*

Card Four: *Root of the Matter.* This card represents the influences and events of the past that have made the querent what he or she is today.

Card Five: *Past Influences.* This is the recent past and the effect it has had on the querent.

Card Six: *Influences in the Near Future.* This card represents any influences that are likely to come into play in the near future.

Card Seven: *Attitude of the Querent.* This card demonstrates how the attitudes of the querent influence circumstances.

Card Eight: *Views of Others.* How others view the querent and the present situation.

Card Nine: *Hopes and Fears.* The inner feelings of the querent.

Card Ten: *The Outcome.* This card reveals the eventual outcome of the influences of the other cards.

Using the Cards for Meditation and Spiritual Development

Each of the seventy-eight tarot cards can be used as a pictorial key or trigger for meditation, and the *Sacred Circle* deck has been designed with this in mind. Each card contains symbols that work on a number of levels that will reveal their complexity and depth with continued study and practice.

Take the card you have decided to work with and study the picture. Examine the border and reflect on what it might mean. Examine the elements that make up the image. Read about the symbolism of the card. When you feel you have the picture and the basic symbolism fixed in your mind, put the card down in front of you, close your eyes, and relax. You are going to enter into the card and interact with it.

For example, suppose you have chosen the Queen of Swords. Imagine the border of the card like an open doorway before you. Within the pillars of the door, gentle winds move clouds around in a blue sky, the power of the element of air in action, though each pillar is mysteriously contained. The cornices are solid and yellow—the magical vibrationary color of the element of air—and carved with an endless knot. You step over the threshold and enter the card.

It is a warm spring day. You feel a breeze and catch on its gentle breath the scents of gorse, bluebell, and primrose flowers, and the sound of bees buzzing through them. It is a day full of promise. From the fresh, white birch trees steps a Lady clad in sunshine yellow. She is the young Spring Goddess. In her right hand, she holds aloft a sword and a hare gambols at her feet. In the wake of her footsteps, flowers emerge from the soft earth and unfold their petals. You may speak to her and she may answer your questions.

You may interact with the scene in any way you wish. Perhaps the Lady will give you a cleansing draft of gorse to purify you and make you ready for what is to come. She may tell you about the sword and what it means, she may present it to you. You may listen to what the bees have to say or you may play with the hare.

You may learn the secrets of the birch or the lessons of the primrose. Spend as long as you like in this magical place.

When you are ready to leave, thank the Lady and any other creature or spirit you have met and feel again the open border behind you. Turn around and step through it. Feel yourself back in your room with the card in front of you and bring yourself back to waking consciousness. When you are ready, open your eyes.

It is a good idea to write down your experience as soon as possible. Keep a record of your meditations and you will be able to perceive any patterns and lessons that are emerging and understand where your path is taking you.

The Journey of the Fool

The Major Arcana is sometimes described as "The Journey of the Fool," charting the progress from the dawning of consciousness to initiation. Each Major Arcana card is meditated on in turn, one each full moon for twenty-two months, using the above technique.

The Green Man

The card of the Green Man represents the energy that triggers the process of dawning consciousness arising from discontent and soul searching, the primal force that the seeker encounters and recognizes at a subconscious level. The Green Man, the raw creative energy of nature, guides the neophyte through the continuous initiation of the seasons and the Wheel of the Year, an unfolding spiral of knowledge and experience.

The High Priest

In this card, the undirected primal energy of the Green Man has begun to take on form. In the Journey, the High Priest card marks the stage where the Fool becomes aware of the fact of his own existence; he comes into consciousness. He begins to think and realizes the power of thought to shape his life. Eventually, he asks himself about the meaning of his life. Psychologically and magically, this card relates to the discovery of the male side of the Self: the *animus*. We all have both male and female aspects within us that must be recognized, accepted, and integrated.

The High Priestess

After becoming aware that he is a conscious being with the power to think and put his thoughts into action, the Fool learns that there is another side to himself, unconnected with the intellect. It is the voice of intuition that recognizes the spirit within. To encounter it, he must surrender himself to the dark womb of the subconscious. Psychologically and magically, the High Priestess represents the feminine side that lies within all of us, man or woman: the *anima*, the instinctive side of our nature as opposed to the rational. The card of the High Priestess is a call to assimilate this into the whole self.

The Lady

After encountering the male and female sides of himself, the Fool now encounters the feminine force of Nature in the form of the Goddess, who nurtures the seed in her earth womb and brings it forth to life and reabsorbs it in death to await another spring. She who is the changeless and ever-changing face of the moon, She who turns the wheel of the stars. The Fool is forced to recognize that there are powers outside himself. He must come to terms with living in a manifest world and learn how to interact with it.

The Lord

After encountering the female force behind Nature, the Fool now encounters the male, in the form of the God, whose seed fertilizes the earth; he whose power is seen reflected in the light of the sun that ripens the crops and illuminates the darkest corners of ignorance. The Fool realizes that there are concerns beyond himself, there are higher forces that are manifest both within himself and the rest of creation. He realizes that he must interact with his environment and with other people, and that he must develop a set of principles and ethics to deal with such concerns. This is part of his spiritual progress.

The Druid

The Fool has encountered the male and female aspects of himself, and the male and female aspects of Nature. He has been made aware of his intellect and his intuition, his physical body, and his spirit. He has learned that he lives in a world of opposites—day and night, summer and winter, male and female, body and spirit. Now from the Druid he learns that these opposites must be balanced in his life. He is neither a purely spiritual being, nor purely a material one, and this duality is part of being human. His task now is to accept and harmonize these aspects within himself and without.

The Lovers

In card six, the Druid, the Fool learned about balancing opposites and polarities. In this card, the Lovers, he learns about the marriage and fusion of those opposites to make a single whole. He becomes aware of the transcendence of the spirit and the development of his eternal soul through the choices he makes.

The Chariot

In the previous card, the Fool met the Lovers and was given a spiritual vision. However, he now learns that this is not enough; he must make his way through the world while he sustains this ideal. He realizes he needs willpower and courage.

The Warrior

At this point, the Fool discovers that he must begin to develop his spiritual Will as opposed to desire or even determination and willpower as exemplified by the Chariot. This involves going deep inside himself to develop his strength by confronting his fears and by following his path boldly, wherever it leads.

The Shaman

This card is usually called The Hermit, from a Greek word meaning *wilderness*. Here the Fool returns to the place where it all began, the greenwood, to commune with the spirits of Nature. He has been taught many lessons by human advisors and been given plenty of advice. Now he feels the need to be alone with Nature to get to the source of things, and cut out the conflicting and clamorous voices of the world of humankind.

After a period of shaking off his conditioning he prepares to take the initiatory drink, a symbol of the initial inward experience. The true initiation begins with a long search for knowledge and many years of study. Then, when the neophyte least expects it, will come an overwhelming vision of wonderful proportions. This will often leave the candidate with a feeling of harmony, belonging, and inviolability that will last for days or weeks. However, this is only the start of the process and there is no turning back.

The Wheel

In the journey of spiritual evolution, which the tarot describes, the Wheel represents the Fool's dawning awareness of the cosmic forces that turn the wheel, the energies of the four elements. The first resonance of the elements is in his own body—earth as bone, air as breath, water as blood, and fire as spirit. The elements flow through the universe, consolidating, dissolving, transforming—a flow of energy that shapes and changes all things in a never-ending cycle. The elements represent different levels of consciousness but they must always be in balance; they are interdependent.

The Web

Here the Fool encounters the Web, the invisible thread that links all life in the cosmos. He realizes that he does not exist or act in isolation, and that on every level he interacts with and affects everything and everyone he comes into contact with. His actions do not only have consequences for himself, but for other people, other creatures, the environment and the planet. He realizes that his past actions have created his present, and present actions will create his future and affect the future of others through the workings of the Web—in both an obvious and a subtle way. Up until this point he has only been concerned with himself, his own consciousness and, latterly, his relationship with Nature. Now he must consider the far-reaching consequences of his relationships and actions.

Sacrifice

With this card, the Fool has come to a realization that he is on the verge of a greater consciousness that cannot be attained by the intellect or by physical action. He must surrender himself to the greater forces of the cosmos and let them do with him as they will. This involves the sacrifice of all that he has previously learned and held sacred, all of his shields and defenses, the things that he has felt have been giving him control over his life and destiny. Here he makes a blind leap into the dark, the unknown, acting on faith alone, hanging suspended between his old self and the new. He is alone, vulnerable and afraid, waiting for what will come.

Death

The Goddess has led the Fool to his death, because only through his spiritual death can he be renewed and come to rebirth. She has asked him to sacrifice his image of himself to find his true Self; the old self must be left behind or "die" before a spiritual rebirth can take place. The frightening Cailleach or Crone is really the Wise Old Woman who guides him. She is the keeper of the mysteries.

Death has stripped the Fool naked in order to go into the Underworld. He can take nothing with him, neither his old securities nor his old beliefs.

The Underworld

The crisis of death has brought the Fool to the gates of the Underworld, where he must journey to the center of the life maze. But
first he must pass the Guardian of the Threshold.

It is the Dark Self that is described as the Guardian of the
Threshold in occult terms, which bars the way to further progress
and ultimately initiation. The Guardian of the Threshold can
adopt terrifying and monstrous forms, which are personifications
of deeply buried fears. Worldwide, shamans and witches describe
the initiatory process as a series of journeys into the Underworld
where fearful monsters must be fought and defeated. It is a frightening thing to be brought face to face with your most severely
repressed fears—something that most would prefer not to do,
would prefer not to know about. However, it is this Dark Self that
opens the gateway to initiation, and the Guardian is not defeated
by repression or being battled with, but by being recognized and
assimilated as part of the whole Self. This whole Self is the treasure the dragon guards.

The Tower

The Fool has undergone his symbolic death and is engaged in his
journey through the Underworld where he seeks the center of the
labyrinth. At the gates of the Underworld, he had to encounter the
Guardian of the Threshold, his subconscious shadow self, which he
had to learn to embrace and assimilate before he could pass. Because
of this, his carefully constructed tower of self-image and protective
delusion collapses and falls, leaving him naked and defenseless, but
for the first time dimly conscious of his whole, True Self.

The collapse of the tower is echoed in descriptions of shamanic
initiation, where the candidate experiences, in a vision, a symbolic
dismemberment whereby his body is stripped down to its bones.

Initiation

In this card, the Fool has reached the center of the labyrinth, where the cauldron of regeneration and rebirth lies. Here he must allow himself to be reabsorbed into the cauldron-womb of the Goddess by dissolving himself in the cauldron, allowing the elements of his being to return to the source and become one with the Goddess once more—free, formless, and unlimited. The Druid Gwion described himself as having been nine months in the womb of Ceridwen before being reborn as Taliesin or "Radiant Brow," meaning *an enlightened one.*

The Star

The Fool has journeyed to the center of the labyrinth, the tower of his false self-image destroyed along the way. After his immersion in the cauldron of inspiration, he now sees a guiding light that will lead him out of the darkness of the Underworld into the full light of his spiritual realization. The Fool is renewed by the Goddess, reformed and reborn, and must now begin the outward journey of the initiation spiral, a difficult journey in which he must absorb and apply the lessons he has learned. The unfolding spiral of his initiation has begun.

The star is often seen as an archetype of the developing True Self; the process of the integration of the ego and the soul at a deeper level of consciousness; the realization of the wholeness and oneness of the mind, body, and spirit—a personal microcosm of the totality of the cosmos.

The Moon

The Fool is engaged in the outward spiral of his initiatory process and has been following the pale light of the star as his guide through the labyrinth. Now he encounters the primordial power of the moon, which calls moisture forth from the earth as refreshing dew, which governs the tides of the oceans that endlessly generate life and reabsorb it in death, and the cycles of women's wombs, readied each month to accept the fertilization of life.

On a magical level, the moon influences and represents the collective sea of the unconscious that contains and feeds all the experiences of humankind, communicated only by symbol and legend. The Fool realizes that though his journey has been an individual one, it is reflected in the journey of all souls; his own experience has contributed to the evolution of humanity as a tiny part of the whole. He has been re-enacting the eternal myth.

The Sun

The Fool has completed his terrifying and perilous journey through the darkness of the Underworld, sustained only by the strength and determination of his spirit. Like all things, his True Self gestated and grew in the dark and strove toward the light. Now the bright light of the sun dispels the shadows and the last of his fears and he is ready to emerge into the daylight world with his new knowledge and his new consciousness.

Rebirth

With this card, the Fool has completed the outward spiral of his initiation: all his lessons have been absorbed. In many ways this was the hardest part of his journey. His world-view was totally altered, and the struggle to center himself in the new consciousness very difficult. Like many new initiates, he experienced confusion, alienation, and depression while the integration took place. His journey from the cauldron has taken several years. Now the unfolding of the initiation into waking consciousness and everyday life has come to fruition and he acts from a new perspective.

The World Tree

The World Tree represents the *axis mundi* or center pole that links all the realms of being and knowledge, and is now centered within the Fool himself. With this card the Fool has ended his journey through the tarot, but now a new one begins.

The Elements

Each of the cards of the four suits of the Minor Arcana can be used to meditate on aspects of the four elements: the cards of the suit of swords are concerned with aspects of mental abilities and the element of air; wands are concerned with aspects of creativity and the element of fire; cups are concerned with aspects of the emotions and the element of water; while the cards of the suit of discs are concerned with aspects of the material plane and the element of earth.

The four elements should be balanced in both the physical and magical worlds of any individual and the cards can be meditated on either individually or in combination. The following exercise can be employed as a regular magical practice to facilitate this.

The Wheel of the Elements

Remove from the deck the four cards representing Air, Fire, Water and Earth and the card representing the World Tree. Lay them out on the floor in front of you with the air card in the east, the fire card in the south, the water card in the west, the earth card in the north, and the world tree card in the center of the circle (below).

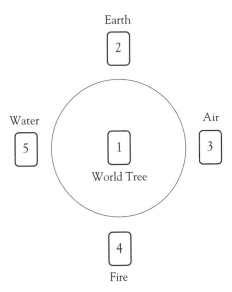

FIGURE 7. *The Wheel of the Elements.*

Choose the element you think you need to work on and seat your-self behind that card. Study the image, then close your eyes and visualize yourself entering the card.

For example, say you think you need to work on your emotions because you find it difficult to express feelings. Seat yourself behind the water card (if you were overly emotional, you would work on developing the element of air). See, in your mind's eye, the borders of the card, free flowing blue water, mysteriously con-tained within pillars, forming an open doorway. Step through the doorway and encounter the plane of the element of water.

Before you, seated on a silver throne, is a kindly man dressed in blue. He is the Lord of the Powers of Water and he welcomes you to his domain. In his right hand he holds a silver cup, brimming with new wine, which he invites you to drink. As you do, the cool, smooth liquid invigorates you, easing away the tensions in your body, and you feel lighter; you move with a new fluid grace.

The King leads you across the hill behind his throne toward the sea shore. The water laps the beach with white-flecked waves, again and again. You hear and feel its rhythm moving within you, and you walk forward and enter the sea. It is warm and you float freely, safe and supported.

Allow yourself to experience the element of water. Feel the movement and pull of the tides, the flow of the waves . . . giving and taking . . . taking and giving . . . .

Feel the power of the sea, from which all life emerged. It is as though you float within the secure waters of your mother's womb and feel the beat of her heart . . . .

Experience the deep pool of your subconscious . . . love and hate . . . daring and cowardice . . . happiness and sorrow . . . .

The water washes over you, cleansing away your negativity, cleansing away your problems, dissolving the blockages that prevent you from experiencing and expressing the flow of your emotions . . . feel the power of water.

When you are ready, leave the sea. You find the King of Water waiting for you. He leads you back to the gateway of pillars. Thank him for his help and turn and walk back through the borders of the card. Open your eyes.

Now imagine that any remaining negativity is draining from you. It travels along a line of power to the center of the circle and is absorbed by the World Tree. See it as a black sludge leaving you and draining through to the roots of the World Tree, where the earth will transform it into positive energy.

The above example concentrates on only one aspect of the element of water. There are numerous others that can be explored.

This exercise can be performed by a group of up to four people together, each choosing one of the elements and seating themselves behind the chosen card and meditating on his or her chosen element. The same format can be used to meditate on the eight festivals, with the cards relating to the festivals placed on the wheel at the quarters and cross-quarters, with the World Tree card, the Initiation card, or the Ace of Cups as the Grail card placed in the center.

Further Meditational Themes of the Cards

Combinations of the cards can be used to work on a number of themes, including those listed below, or you can choose suitable cards to explore themes of your own.

Aspects of the Goddess

The Lady, The Lovers, The Web, Death, The Cauldron, The Moon, Queen of Swords, Queen of Wands, Queen of Cups, Queen of Discs†

Aspects of the God

The Green Man, The Lord, The Lovers, Sacrifice, The Underworld, The Sun, King of Swords, King of Wands, King of Cups, King of Discs†

---

†The elemental aspects of the four kings and queens should be disregarded in this instance.

The Seasons

Spring: Page of Swords, Queen of Swords, King of Swords

Summer: Ace of Wands, Page of Wands, Queen of Wands, King of Wands

Autumn: Ace of Cups, Three of Cups, Queen of Cups, King of Cups

Winter: Knight of Discs, Queen of Discs, King of Discs

The Eight Festivals

Samhain: Underworld, The Shaman, The Tower, Initiation

Yule: Rebirth, Ace of Discs, King of Discs

Imbolc: Moon, High Priestess

Ostara: The Lady, The Lord, Queen of Swords, King of Swords

Beltane: The Lovers, The Green Man

Coamhain: The High Priest, Sun, Queen of Wands, King of Wands

Lughnasa: Warrior

Herfest: Death, Sacrifice, Ace of Cups, Queen of Cups

The Wheel of the Year: The Wheel

The Holly King and The Oak King:
The battle of summer and winter

The Green Man, The King of Discs, the King of Wands

Other Combinations

A wide variety of other combinations is possible. For example, it is possible to study all the cards that depict animals to study animal lore, or all the cards that contain plants and trees to study Herb Craft. Polarities may be studied by pairing The Lord and Lady, The Sun and Moon, cards representing summer and winter, spring and autumn, and so on. With time and thought you will soon be able to put together card combinations to suit your own purposes and needs.

The Arrows of Brighid

The Goddess Brighid was said to possess three fiery arrows of inspiration, related to her attributes as Goddess of poetry, the hearth or forge fire, and the healing flame. These are associated, by some authorities, with the sign of Awen, said to be the name that the universe calls God, formed of the letters O (the circle of Gwynwyd, perfection and completion, the superconscious, the spirit or heavens), I (Abred, the physical plane, the world in which we live), and U (the cauldron of Annwn, which underlies the manifest world, the cauldron of rebirth and inspiration, the subconscious or unconscious, the Underworld). The three letters can also be said to represent earth, sea, and air; love, wisdom, and truth; or mind, body, and spirit.

The layout described in figure 8 (below) is used to divine the deeper nature of your personal and spiritual progress. Each card

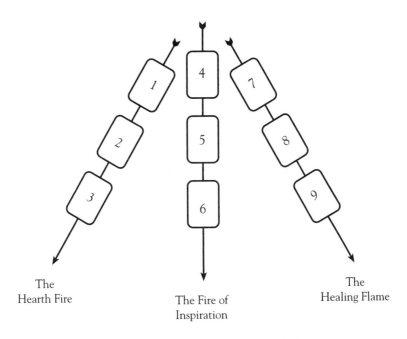

The
Hearth Fire

The Fire of
Inspiration

The
Healing Flame

FIGURE 8. *The Arrows of Brighid.*

that appears should then be meditated on in combination with the other cards that appear on the same "arrow."

The Hearth Fire (cards one, two, three): These cards reflect your current home situation and close relationships and may give advice on how to improve matters.

The Fire of Inspiration (cards four, five, six): These cards reflect the sources of creative and spiritual inspiration.

The Fire of Healing (cards seven, eight, and nine): These cards show what needs healing and may give advice on how that healing is best obtained.

Major Arcana

The Journey of the Fool

The Green Man

The card shows the Green Man. Made up from many different kinds of leaves, acorns, and pine cones, he strides through the wildwood, the incarnation of its spirit.

The Symbolism

The Green Man is the vegetation spirit of the wildwood. Perhaps the most tenacious Pagan god of all, his image survives in church carvings and pub signs all over Britain, in which he is usually depicted in the form of a severed head with branches and leaves emerging from the mouth. A strange figure—half man, half tree.

At one time, most of Britain was covered with forest, and there are many legends of forest spirits called wood woses, faery wildfolk, green men, or wild men. Those who saw them described them as green people, powerful spirits who could sometimes be appealed to for help and had to be placated if they were angered—their elf bolts or flint arrows were deadly. The wise ones knew that forest spirits used certain natural features of the landscape as power places to manifest themselves—such as particular wells, streams, rocks, and trees—and would leave gifts at these places for them. These Green Spirits represent the raw, untamed, primal force of nature—a somewhat frightening concept to the modern mind, which prefers nature safe, controlled, and "civilized."

The green-clad wildmen passed into lore as fairies, often given the name of Hob, Robin, or Robin Goodfellow; this is the real Pagan origin of Robin Hood, who has far more mythological significance than the outlaw who robbed the rich to give to the poor and fought the evil sheriff of Nottingham. The clues to his identity lie in his name, his green clothing, his forest home, and his deadly arrows; he was the nature god of the ordinary people who could seek him in the forest. A depiction of Robin and his men at the fourteenth-century chapter house at Southwell Minster in Nottinghamshire shows them as twelve green men merging with various sacred plants such as hawthorn and ivy. In the Traditional Craft, the Lord is often addressed as Robin and the Lady as Marion.

The concept of the Green Man also appears in the Arthurian story of Sir Gawain and the Green Knight:

As Arthur and his court were celebrating Yule, the great doors of the feasting hall flew open and in rode a knight, entirely green from head to foot. In a loud voice, he issued a challenge to the company—was anyone brave enough to take the axe he carried and chop off his head, which compliment he would return in a year's time?

Puzzled by his request, the knights merely stared and the mysterious Green Knight chided them as cowards. Stung by this, Sir Gawain leaped up, seized the axe, and cut off the knight's head. To everyone's amazement, the Green Knight merely picked up his head and bid Gawain to meet him in a year's time at the Green Chapel.

A year passed and Gawain rode off with a heavy heart in search of the Green Chapel. He traveled far and wide, but was unable to find anyone who had even heard of it. Eventually, he came to a castle that was preparing to celebrate the Yuletide season. The Lord of the manor, a big, jovial, red-headed man, made him welcome and admitted he knew where the chapel was—a short ride from his estate. However, as there were still three days to go until the appointment, he invited the knight to remain with his wife and himself until the time should come. Gawain readily agreed.

Each day Gawain hunted with the Red Lord, but each night the Lord's wife came to his room to try to seduce him. Being an honorable knight, Gawain refused. But on the last night, the lady came to him with a magic green garter, which she said she would exchange for a kiss. She claimed the garter had the quality of protecting its wearer from any kind of weapon. Seeing a chance to save his life for no more than a kiss, the bargain was made, the lady kissed, and the garter taken.

The next day, Gawain set off to the Green Chapel, a cave in the woodlands. The Green Knight stepped out to meet him and asked if he was ready to lose his head. Gawain meekly kneeled before him and bowed his head. The Green Knight raised the axe high and brought it down, but stopped just short of the neck of Gawain, who couldn't help flinching. Ashamed of his cowardice, he apologized and bid the knight strike again. Once again the axe came down and stopped short, but Gawain held himself steady. Raising the axe once more the Knight struck, merely nicking Gawain's neck.

Gawain looked up, and instead of the Green Knight, there stood his host, the Red Lord. The Lord praised his courage in meeting the challenge and said that the two blows that didn't touch him were in reward for his constancy in refusing the seductions of the lady of the castle. The third blow, which had cut him, was for giving in to temptation and kissing the lady. Embracing each other, they returned to the castle to celebrate the twelve days of Yule, and it was a strange tale that Gawain had to tell when he returned to Arthur's court.

This is a very ancient story, with the Green Knight representing the power of Nature and the Old Religion. He is the Holly King, anciently believed to fight a twice-yearly battle with the Oak King for the hand of the Goddess and the rulership of six months of the year, the Holly King ruling the waning year and the Oak King the waxing.

The Vegetation Spirit makes an appearance to this day in folklore festivals associated with May Day. Here he is Jack-in-the-Green or the May King, played by a man wreathed in oak and hawthorn with only his face showing. In pantomime, he enacts a death scene before springing to life to dance with the May Queen, symbolizing the death of winter and the yearly renewal of fertility with the coming of the warm days of summer.

Divinatory Meanings

The Green Man is the raw power of Nature, untamed energy, the wild and fertile force behind all natural growth. He can be seen as the Divine impulse of creation, which is not under the control of man: the primal chaos from which matter crystallizes and order emerges. In the past, this force was respected and honored, and people strove to work in harmony with nature, to live within its cycles and become part of them. Today humankind, as a species, has lost respect for nature and seeks to control and defeat it. We now know that this is causing dire consequences not only for our planet, but for our spiritual well-being. We, too, are natural beings.

Robin Hood was, and is, a force that exists outside of manmade society, refusing to be governed by its rules and conventions, fighting its injustices and wrongs. Such a character is often seen as dangerous or even mad because he doesn't conform, though throughout history such characters have sown the seeds of change with new ideas—scientists ahead of their time, philosophers, artists, visionaries, and revolutionaries—people often ridiculed and sometimes persecuted in their own lifetimes.

If the Green Man appears in your spread, it indicates that powerful forces are at work in your life breaking down the old order so that a new one may emerge. You may have been feeling restless and discontented and have an overwhelming impulse to throw away everything you have worked for to seek new experiences and new horizons, without any clear idea of what these will be. This course of action will inevitably lead to a period of chaos and you will leave behind some old friends and relationships. However, you will meet new people and begin a new phase of existence in which you will learn and grow immeasurably. Trust in your instincts and the new pattern of your life will eventually emerge from the chaos and become clear.

Spiritually you will receive unexpected guidance and fresh inspiration with experiences far beyond the usual. It is the call of the Otherworld to seek and know. Precisely what you seek is not yet clear—you may greet the call with a mixture of excitement and anxiety; it is a leap into the dark.

Reverse Meanings

You are afraid to take risks, preferring to cling to what you know, whether this makes you happy or not. Your life may be boring, but you are too cautious to make a change, instead you settle down into a drab existence while things pass you by. Remember, it is not what you do in life that you will regret, but what you don't do—the opportunities missed. Do you really want to let life pass you by? Nothing is gained without risk. A risk is a risk, and you might fail, but at least you will have tried, you will have experienced, you will have learned from it.

The Journey of the Fool

The Major Arcana is sometimes described as "the journey of the fool," charting the progress of the spirit toward initiation. The Green Man is the force that triggers the process, arising from discontent and soul searching, the primal force that the seeker encounters and recognizes at a subconscious level. He guides the neophyte through the initiation of the seasons and the Wheel of the Year, an unfolding spiral of knowledge and experience.

The High Priest

The card depicts the High Priest, a distinguished man clad in golden robes. Around his brow he wears a golden fillet emblazoned with a sun disc, and in his hands he clasps a book, the cover of which is inscribed with a pentacle. He stands in a summer meadow—chamomile, fennel, fern, mint, marigold, and yarrow grow at his feet, an ash tree stands behind him. The summer solstice sun stands at noon, high in the sky.

The Symbolism

The high priest is a man of religion who interprets received and written knowledge and passes on his findings to his pupils. He represents the use of the intellect, the logical mind, the power of thought to shape existence. He is a philosopher who uses his mind to interpret the world around him, to think about his purpose and what it all means. To this end, he delves into books of philosophy, religion, science, and magic in an attempt to understand.

He is shown standing in a bright summer meadow at the time of the summer solstice, which we call Coamhain. This is a time of glory when the days are long, the weather is warm, and plant and animal life flourishes. At his feet grow some of the sacred herbs of midsummer, which at this time are imbued with greater magical value and are gathered for protection and purification. Of particular interest to him might be the mint, which means "thought" and is used to stimulate mental activity. Possibly he is consulting his book to determine this.

Behind him is the ash tree, which was sacred to our ancestors who would cut ash wands on midsummer eve to attract inspirational fire from the heavens. The word *ash* means "great fire blaze" as the ash, like the oak, seems to attract lightning. The ancients saw the lightning as the fertilizing force of the Sky God striking Mother Earth from the heavens. The ash was one of the channels attracting the lightning from the sky, through the tree, down into the womb of the earth, and through its roots. Because the ash links all the realms, it is used as the shaft of the witch's broomstick to conduct magical energy.

Divinatory Meanings

Your thoughts turn inward and you become more concerned with who you are and where you are going rather than with putting plans into action. To work in any area of life, but especially in areas of psychic and personal development, the most important thing is, as the ancients dictated, to "know thyself." This means understanding what makes you what you are, forgiving yourself for your mistakes, and learning to like yourself. When you accomplish this, you can learn not to make the same mistakes over and over again, to utilize all your potentials and become whatever you want to be—whatever that may be. What the world tells you that you should be, and what you want to be may be two very different things.

If the card of the High Priest appears in your spread, it is telling you that you have unexplored skills and abilities. The High Priest is telling you that you must organize, plan, and use the creative power of your mind to achieve your full potential. It is through your thoughts that you interpret your past, understand your present, and shape your future.

What would you like to do, more than anything else, in life? Are you working toward it? Everyone has something they have always wanted to do, but have put it off or just thought they couldn't do it. It could be a special trip, a career change, a creative project, or learning a new skill. Give yourself the chance. Make a plan to deal with it. Remember that your deepest longing is sometimes the thing you have come into this life to do. Start now, tonight. Explore what it would take and begin. It may take a long time to get there, but if you don't start the journey you never will arrive.

On a spiritual level, the High Priest is the inner guide whose voice is sometimes obscured by the confusion of your thoughts and the tumult of events, but which nevertheless is always present, perhaps guiding you subconsciously to what you need through a chance meeting, a book you happen to read, or even a dream. Deep within yourself, you have unknown strengths and abilities to explore and develop. You are seeking answers to philosophical questions and you may be drawn to study a philosophy or religion in the hope that it may have the answers.

Reverse Meanings

You find it difficult to express yourself—perhaps you think no one will be interested in what you have to say. You need to work on your self-image; you are lacking in confidence and constantly put yourself down. What is it that makes you this way? Perhaps in the past the people criticized you and didn't appreciate your talents. You have developed a habitual negative response to situations, which is not helping you to solve your problems. You tend to react to situations with feelings of anger and helplessness. These negative thought patterns are standing in the way of your development and happiness—you must learn to let them go. You may need the help of another to do this, perhaps a counselor, therapist, or spiritual advisor, or even a superior at work. Look at yourself as you are now; you have a lot to offer. Perhaps in the past other people helped to destroy your confidence, but only you are responsible now for what you feel, what you do. Take responsibility for yourself and shape yourself into the person you want to be.

The Journey of the Fool

In this card, the primal energy of the Green Man has begun to take on form.

In the journey of the fool, the High Priest card marks the stage when the fool becomes aware of the fact of his own existence; he comes into consciousness. He begins to think and realizes the power of thought to shape his life. Eventually, he asks himself about the meaning of his life. As he moves toward his meeting with the High Priestess, this newly realized consciousness begins to seek the spirit within.

Psychologically and magically, this card relates to the discovery of the male side of the Self, the *animus*. We all have both male and female aspects within us which must be recognized, accepted, and integrated.

The High Priestess

This card depicts the High Priestess, a pale and serious woman clad in white and silver robes. On her forehead she wears a silver fillet bearing the image of a crescent moon. In her hand she holds a crystal ball. She is shown standing beside a holy well accompanied by a swan. Behind her in the sky is a full moon and a willow branch overhangs the border. Snowdrops grow at her feet, demonstrating that it is the season when the first signs of spring begin to stir—the festival of Imbolc, which falls at the beginning of February.

The Symbolism

The High Priestess is the witch, the Wise Woman who relies on her intuitive understanding to gain wisdom. She knows the cycles of nature, the patterns of the stars, the tides of the moon, the habits of the animals, and the virtues of every plant.

For the ancients, the earth was sacred and the source of all knowledge. It was the body of the Goddess herself. She was the land, and the landscape contained entrances to her secret inner realms, her womb, often called the Underworld. These were hollows in the earth—such as caves, springs, and wells—which were holy, and veneration of them still persists. Such wells were believed to have healing powers and were presided over by Pagan deities, many of whom were later transformed into Christian saints, such as Brighid, or passed into folklore as "white ladies" or "green ladies." Gifts of colored rags, pins, and garlands would be left at the wells to solicit healing from its resident spirit. Even today, people throw coins into "wishing" wells.

The festival of Brighid, or Brigantia, is Imbolc, when we celebrate the Goddess returning renewed after the winter dark, and all things feminine. In Irish legend, Brighid was a triple fire goddess whose name means "fiery arrow." Hers are the three fire arrows of inspiration, healing, and the hearthfire or forge. She is the muse of poets, the goddess of healing wells, and the patroness of the magician smith who transformed, by his alchemy, elements of the Underworld into beautiful or useful objects. Brighid carries a white wand with which she regenerates the lifeless land.

In this card, a willow tree hangs over Brighid's well. The willow is sacred to the Moon Goddess because it is a tree that loves water, and the moon governs the tides and brings moisture in the form of dew. The sea, the emotions, and the feminine are governed by the moon, which, in its monthly rhythm, is female, as opposed to the daily movements of the sun, which is considered male. The word *witch* is derived from the word for willow. The witch's besom is made of an ash stake, birch twigs, and a willow binding. As a tree of the Moon Goddess, willow strengthens the intuition and gives inspiration, paving the way to knowledge.

Brighid's bird familiar, the swan, circles the well. It was once believed that a swan only sings once—when it is dying. Its song is associated with prophecy (knowing its own death), music, and poetry. Swan skin and feathers were used to make the cloak of a Celtic poet. In some stories, the song of a swan held magical properties that could make mortals sleep.

Divinatory Meanings

The card of the High Priestess represents a link to the subconscious mind, the inner world of the Self, which cannot be accessed through the intellect or waking consciousness, but which is only revealed in dreams and symbols. It is like the Underworld womb of the Goddess, in which seeds are planted and grow toward the light—its hidden workings shape the underlying personality and responses of an individual, which become manifest in the everyday world. This card is telling you to pay attention to your dreams and intuitions; a facet of you is trying to make itself known.

When this card appears in a spread, it indicates that your life is changing. Things that once seemed so certain can no longer be taken for granted. Some puzzling mysteries become more clear, but all is not yet revealed at this point. On the bonus side, you will find that your intuitive powers are increasing and you may be inspired to be creative; this is a particularly good card for poets and writers. Depending on the surrounding cards, the High Priestess can mean that a noble and gentle influence will enter your life in the form of a woman, either as a friend or a lover.

Spiritually you are about to attain a new level of enlightenment. You may have realized the power of your intuition and have begun to study psychic matters. This card can indicate a particular attraction to the occult, a thirst for secret knowledge. At this point, you must pay attention to the lesson of the swan. She is a guide to the Otherworld consciousness, parting the swan-veil mist to allow access. Swan is telling you that knowledge will not come at this time through action or intellectual endeavor, but by listening to the inner voice of the spirit, which may be missed in the hurly-burly of chatter and business. Put aside times of silence when you can become aware and listen.

Reverse Meanings

If this card appears reversed in your spread, it can indicate that you have been gaining occult knowledge on a superficial level without any comprehension of its true significance, perhaps merely to impress others. It can also indicate that you have not been listening to your intuition or have been trying to ignore something that you know deep down is true; in either case this will cause problems for you.

On a deeper level, the High Priestess reversed can mean that you have failed to come to terms with yourself as a woman. If you are a man, it can indicate a damaging refusal to accept the feminine, emotional, intuitive side of yourself.

The Journey of the Fool

After becoming aware that he is a conscious being with the power to think and put his thoughts into action, the fool learns that there is another side to himself, unconnected with the intellect. It is the voice of intuition that recognizes the spirit within. To encounter it, he must surrender to the dark womb of the subconscious.

Psychologically and magically, the High Priestess represents the feminine side that lies within all of us, man or woman—the *anima*, the instinctive side of our nature, as opposed to the rational. The card of the High Priestess is a call to assimilate this into the whole self.

The Lady

This card depicts the Goddess as Earth Mother or Mother Nature. She wears a blood red dress and holds in her arms a cornucopia from which tumble the good things of the harvest, her bounty. She is crowned with a circlet of stars and stands in a meadow while a hare frolics at her feet through primroses, violets, daisies, bluebells and marigolds. The sun and the moon are both visible in the sky behind her. The top border of the card shows an apple bough, on which the blossom, bud, and fruit appear at the same time. Bees hover along the border of the card.

The Symbolism

The Lady is the Goddess, the feminine energy behind manifest nature, the bestower of fertility and creativity who brings all seeds to fruition. Humankind's earliest deity was the Great Mother, who gave birth to the cosmos and nourished it with her milk. Even the distant stars were seen as drops of milk from her breasts, hence the name of the Milky Way. Our ancestors saw themselves as part of nature, children of the Great Mother, along with the earth, the heavens, the animals, and the plants that existed alongside them. Creation was related in a single whole, a difficult concept for modern human, but one we in the Craft try to recapture.

The Lady is the mother of all things. Seeds are sown in her earth womb, she brings them to life and nurtures them into growth; from this bounty men and animals are fed and nourished. She presides over the whole cycle of being—planting, growth, and harvest. She is the bringer of life, death, and rebirth. At the harvest, the seeds and the dead are laid back into her womb so that she may bring them to yet another cycle.

For many thousands of years the Goddess was seen as the single source, one capable of constantly generating and regenerating without the aid of any outside agency. This is the original meaning of the word *virgin*. The Great Goddess is often pictured as a queen bee, as it was once believed that bees were self-fertilizing, and were therefore associated with virginity. The Romans believed that bee keepers should be celibate, and legend has it that bees will not sting a virgin.

The apple bough in the border of the card represents immortality, the passage of time, the turning of the wheel, and the mysteries of the Goddess. When cut in half, an apple shows the pentacle at its heart, containing the seeds. Five is one of the sacred numbers of the Goddess, symbolizing the five senses; the five ages of man; the five stations in Her year—birth, initiation, consummation, repose, and death. The apple tree may also be seen as having five stations in the year—the blossom in spring; ripe fruit at Lughnasa; as a symbol of the setting sun in the west at the point of the autumn equinox; at Samhain, the journey through the Underworld, contact with the other worlds, divination, and intuition; and the bare tree being wassailed at midwinter, the time of the sun's rebirth and the promise of the waxing year to come.

Several traditions have a myth connecting the Tree of Knowledge with the fall of man from the innocence of the primordial state into the dualistic world and self-consciousness. On the other hand, eating the fruit of the Tree of Life can confer immortality (through the cycle of death and rebirth), and restore man to the lost paradise of wholeness and connection through initiation into the mysteries of the Goddess. Bran, in Celtic myth, was summoned by the Goddess to enter the Land of Youth with a "silver white blossomed branch from Emain, in which the bloom and branch were one."

The hill in the picture is Silbury Hill, near Avebury in Wiltshire. It was constructed about 4,600 years ago and represents the womb of the Goddess. Originally, a water-filled trench surrounded it. The full moon in late July or early August (Lughnasa) would be reflected in the waters so that it appeared a child's head was emerging from the womb. As the moon moved up through the sky it appeared reflected at the breast of the image, as though suckling. As the moon moved higher, the "milk" was released from the breast as the moat reflected the moonlight. With the cutting of the umbilical cord, the signal was given to begin the harvest.

Divinatory Meanings

The card of the Lady represents mothering in its widest sense. It is telling you that you must recognize that your spirit lives within nature, you are a child of the earth and should seek to care for and respect your fellow beings and the environment. It is important to connect with the earth and with reality, or, in magical terms, to be grounded. Your body is a precious gift of the Mother, one that enables you to experience the beauties of the world and the simple pleasures of life. The card speaks of the wisdom in recognizing that all the cycles of life are equally valid, that all things have their season. This involves recognizing the time to act and the time to wait patiently for things to mature.

If this card appears in your spread, it heralds a harmonious and successful phase in your life, full of beauty and pleasure. You may be expecting a child, or perhaps you have begun a new creative project. Relationships with family and friends are happy and loving. The Lady also indicates good health.

Spiritually, this is a time of great creativity and progress, especially if you coordinate with the efforts of others. It heralds a moment of connection with the Goddess, of being tangibly aware of her love and spiritual nourishment.

Reverse Meanings

If the Lady appears reversed in your spread, it demonstrates your unwillingness to recognize the cycles of change—you are trying to hold onto what is already passing away. You are preventing your own growth with these attitudes—your creativity is blocked and your spirit is stagnating.

If you have domestic problems with children or partners, you must look to your own behavior for the cause. You may be unreasonably possessive in your relationships and not allowing your loved ones to change and grow through fear of losing them, although it is precisely these restrictions that are pushing them away.

Depending on the surrounding cards, the Lady reversed can indicate problems with your fertility—either sterility or infertility—or an unwanted pregnancy. It can also demonstrate a promiscuity that comes from seeking out sexual relationships for sensation alone, rather than love, perhaps through fear of commitment.

The Journey of the Fool

After encountering the male and female sides of himself, the fool now encounters the feminine force of nature. He is forced to recognize that there are powers outside of himself. He must come to terms with living in a manifest world and learn how to interact responsibly with it.

The Lord

As the card of the Lady shows the feminine force of nature, the card of the Lord shows the masculine, which the ancients depicted as a horned being. He stands, leaning on his staff, in a forest clearing. It is early summer and leaves appear on the apple, hawthorn, elder, birch, honeysuckle, and oak. Gathered around him, their rivalry forgotten under his benign influence, are some of the animals of the woodland—the stag, the hare, and the badger.

The Symbolism

The earliest known representation of a god is the Lord of the Animals, a horned figure depicted in cave paintings with a variety of animals and hunting scenes. The animals are shown in symbolic relationship to each other and to man, demonstrating that life is interconnected and interdependent. Real animals were a mere reflection of their spirit archetypes. Hunting and killing were mystical as well as practical experiences. Life, of necessity, preys on life; this is a mystery in itself and was celebrated in a sacred manner. Life would be reverenced as it was taken. In the world of the hunter-gatherer, people were forced to hunt and kill their animal neighbors, thus taking their spirit. For this it was necessary to make ritual restitution. Blood and fat were mixed with the painting pigments—the paintings thus uniting the spirit and material planes. With the painting and the blood, the animal spirit was returned to the earth womb (cave).

It is often said that various religious cultures have "worshiped animals," particularly so-called "primitive" tribes. This is to misunderstand the complex relationship that exists in such cultures with the environment, its animals, and its plants. Animals' powers are never worshiped, but often represent certain forces or attributes seen as intrinsic to the balance of the environment and the cosmos. We know that in every tribal society, including ones that still exist, animals were considered to have particular virtues and abilities.

Celtic art is rich with depictions of animals. Tribal names were derived from animal totems such as the Epidii (horse), the Lugi (raven), and the Tochrad (boar). Mythological characters were described as having their destinies bound up with the fate of certain animals. Celtic gods and goddesses were said to turn into animals, to have animal companions, and to gain knowledge from talking to animals. Druids were credited with similar abilities, while animal herdsmen were often also magicians. Celtic gods were described as being nearly always accompanied by their cult animal or appearing as an animal—stag, horse, dog, and so forth. The Lord of the Animals, sometimes called Cernunnos, is a horned figure surrounded by animals—just like the figures that appear in the cave paintings.

We know, from the many carvings that have been preserved, that the Celts had a horned god. It is likely that he was a fertility and hunting god of the ordinary people, rather than of the priesthood and intelligentsia, as his names and legends do not come down to us. He is generally called Cernunnos from a single inscription on a carving in Gaul, probably a Latinized version of a Celtic name. In Britain he may have been called Kern or Herne, as legends of a horned figure called Herne are associated with Windsor Great Park. A figure is still said to haunt the park, riding out with the Wild Hunt at the midwinter solstice. He is described as a mighty, bearded figure with a huge pair of stag's horns on his head. He wears chains, carries a hunting horn, and rides out on a black horse with a pack of ferocious hunting hounds. His name may have been discerned from the call that the hind makes to the stag in the mating season—*Hh-ern*. From the depiction of the Horned God, he is clearly the Lord of the Animals, always shown in the company of various beasts. He is sometimes shown as holding a serpent and a torc, showing that he is a god of winter and summer, sky and Underworld, death and resurrection.

The stag was one of the four sacred animals of the Celts and is prominent in British and Irish myth. Stags clean their new antlers in August and September, rubbing off their velvety coating onto the branches of trees. The rutting season begins then, often going on into November, driven to greater ferocity by the frosts. Perhaps for this reason, the stag is associated with the Otherworld and rules over winter the festivals of Samhain and the midwinter solstice. During the winter, the stag herds are said to be protected by the Cailleach, or Hag Goddess, and her women, who herd and milk them.

In Arthurian legend, the knights would take part in a yearly hunt of the white stag, and its head would be presented to the fairest lady in the land. This is probably a seasonal tale of the battle between summer and winter. It was once thought that the "King Stag," leader of the herd, should be ritually hunted and killed every year to ensure the return of summer. The king or royal stag was a beast with twelve or fourteen points on his horns—a stag would have to have been seven years old to have twelve points. The Taliesin poem states "I am a stag of seven tines"— seven points on each horn—seven tines represent the seven lunar months from the winter solstice to the summer solstice.

Horned beasts were generally considered sacred, the horns a symbol of fertility. Antlers were among the earliest tools used to till the soil, and powdered stag antlers are among the best fertilizers known to man.

Divinatory Meanings

The card of the Lord reflects the concept of fatherhood in its widest sense. The Lord tells us the earth is a place of beauty, an earthly paradise, unless we ourselves destroy it. It is not a place of evil from which the spirit must escape, but rather the place where the spirit learns and flourishes. All things have their place and purpose. The spirit should not seek to escape, but instead seek to learn its place and purpose.

This card indicates that the time has come for you to reassess your moral values and ethical codes. If you have merely gone along with the people around you, it is time to take a stand and regain your self-respect. You must rely on yourself and your own judgment. You are called upon to demonstrate authority and qualities of leadership, to act effectively in the world, perhaps to defend some important principle against a powerful individual or corporation.

If the Lord appears in your spread, it heralds a time of great energy and activity when you will be engaged in making something manifest in the world, whether it is a family, a building, a business enterprise, or a work of art. You will be able to call on the knowledge and experience that you have gained to achieve your ambition.

Spiritually, you are called upon to stand on your own two feet, to formulate your own ideas and principles, rather than being led by others. The Horned God is both Lord of the Animals and Herne the Hunter. In the context of the tarot, the question is "What is it that the hunter hunts?" The answer: his own Self. In many myths, a mysterious white hart appears to the hero, challenging him to hunt it through the forest. It may lead the hero into the Otherworld. The stag turns out to be his own soul, and the hunt a necessary lesson.

The Lord of the Animals was associated with the annual cull of the herds, a process of purification to clear away the old growth in order to make way for the new. He is a sacrificial God, giving up the life of the stag for the good of the many, representing growth through sacrifice. The fate of the white stag symbolizes the soul growth that requires radical changes on all levels of consciousness. The spiritual hunter seeks to develop those qualities within himself that will further his development: unwavering concentration on the object in hand, attention to detail, single mindedness, a quest for the truth, the courage to pursue his quarry, and knowing what his quarry is. Concentration rates as the first of the eightfold ways of making magic in the Craft; it is a fundamental quality that must be developed by anyone seeking to develop themselves and their consciousness.

Reverse Meanings

If the Lord card appears reversed in your spread, it often indicates that you lack self-control, ambition, and the ability to deal with any kind of authority. In fact, you probably show contempt for any kind of order. This demonstrates a lack of self-respect, possibly stemming from a problematic relationship with a father figure (not necessarily your father) or a smothering relationship with a parent that you are unable to escape, even if that parent is now dead. Are you going to allow yourself to remain in bondage to the past for the rest of your life? Or are you going to resolve the relationship and move forward? The choice is yours and no one else's.

The reverse of the benign Lord of the Animals who is prepared to sacrifice himself for the good of others is the petty tyrant who tries to dominate others with his rigid rules and inflexible principles that take no account of human feeling and crushes the life spirit from those under his influence. You are being asked to examine whether you are in danger of becoming such a person or whether you have fallen under the influence of one. You cannot grow or even breathe freely under such restrictions and you must break free.

The Journey of the Fool

After encountering the female force behind nature, the fool now encounters the male in the form of the God. He realizes that to act within the world he must develop his own set of ethics and principles, precisely because he knows that there are concerns beyond his own selfish ones and he must interact with his environment and other people. He understands that there are higher forces manifest both within himself and the rest of creation, and that dealing with others according to his ideals is part of his spiritual progress.

The Druid

The card shows a druid on the evening of the midwinter solstice, which we call Yule. He wears a garland of oak and holly leaves. A wren perches on one corner of the card, and a robin on the chalice. The dawn sun rises behind him through the stones of Stonehenge.

Before him is a stone altar on which are his tools—a wand, a sword, a cup, and a disc—which represent the four elements.

The Symbolism

The Druids were the Celtic priesthood and were accorded such a high status that they were equivalent to the first rank of nobles. Both men and women could become Druids, and they not only officiated at magical and religious ceremonies, but were teachers, healers, seers, and storytellers, as well as having judicial functions. Their teachings were passed on orally through learning verses, riddles, and stories. The training of a Druid took many years, passing through three grades—the bard, the vate, and finally the Druid.

Here the Druid is shown standing at a stone altar, on which are placed four of his tools: a sword, representing air and the strength of his intellect; a wand, representing fire and the power of his will; a cup, representing water and his emotions; and a disc or pentacle, representing the earth and his physical body.

Stonehenge was once quite wrongly thought to be a Druid temple; it predates their activity in Britain by some 2,000 years. Its construction probably began around 3300 B.C.E. and was finished in its present form around 1800 B.C.E. It is a ritual observatory, oriented to the midsummer sunrise. However, the Druids probably took over the ritual sites of the aboriginal peoples of Britain, and as far as we can tell, midsummer festivities have been held at Stonehenge almost continually from ancient to modern times.

When Stonehenge was built, the first ray of the midsummer sun would have been in line with the axis of the henge, rising between the Heel Stone and its missing companion. This axis extended in a landscape line to link with two Iron Age earthworks some miles distant: Sidbury Hill on one side and Grovely Castle on the other. However, the stones not only mark the position of the summer solstice dawn, but a diagonal across the Station Stone gives the sunrises and sunsets on the cross-quarter days and both the midwinter sunset and the equinox moonrises are indicated.

The robin and the wren are the totem birds of winter and summer, alternate rulers of six months of the year—in folklore they are sometimes said to be husband and wife. Both birds are also said to have been instrumental in bringing fire to humankind from the sun—the robin burned its breast, making it red, by throwing itself onto the wren to stifle the flames that were burning it. The wren was also scorched by the sun, but in gratitude the other birds all gave a feather to renew his plumage, except the owl who refused. This is why the wren is such an untidy looking bird.

The robin is associated with fire, particularly the fire of the sun at the winter solstice. Its red breast marks it as a fire bird in the midst of winter, like the red berries of the evergreen holly. It is a bird of the dark half of the year, a totem of the Holly King that undergoes a symbolic battle with the wren, totem of the Oak King, at the winter solstice. As a familiar, Robin presides over rituals connected with fire and with initiations through fire, speaking of the persistence of spirit and of light in darkness.

Wren ceremonies were enacted up to the nineteenth century and may well have dated from the Megalithic Age. These ceremonies were conducted around the midwinter solstice, when rituals were performed to chase away the powers of darkness. The wren represented the death and rebirth of the sun at the winter solstice. In ogham its name is *druen*, related to *dur* or *oak*, ruler of the light half of the year. Wren is the totem bird of the Oak King, ruler of the light half of the year in opposition to the Holly King and his totem the robin, rulers of the dark half of the year. As a familiar, Wren knows the mysteries of the turning of the wheel and is privy to all the Druids knew.

Among the ancient peoples, the winter was the time of dark, cold, and death, a time when the darker forces were in ascendance. The holly is evergreen and lasts throughout the winter, representing continuing life, though it is thorny and difficult. The red berries may represent blood and sacrifice, or perhaps the blood and light of the Sun God, believed to be reborn at the midwinter solstice. The holly's place in the ogham alphabet is *tinne*, meaning *fire*.

In ogham the oak is *duir*, meaning *door* in Gaelic. The word for door and oak, and perhaps Druid, come from the same root in many European languages, perhaps because a door made from oak offers protection and solidity and because oaks often marked boundaries; or perhaps because the oak is the door to knowledge and marks boundaries of a different kind. The oak flowers at midsummer and marks the door opening on one side to the waxing and on the other to the waning year. It stands at the turning of the year.

Divinatory Meanings

The Druid is the spiritual teacher within you who recognizes the necessity of opposites in balance. This card emphasizes the need to bring into harmony your relationship with the material world and the ordinary consciousness and the realm of spirit. Every person's experience of the Divine is different and every individual must work through their spiritual development in their own way. The Druid within tells you that you must define your own balance, it cannot be achieved by following dogma or set practices.

If the card of the Druid appears in your spread, it indicates that new opportunities will arise for you and you will have the chance to put your ideas into practice. This will give you a chance to demonstrate your expertise and give your confidence a huge boost. The card may herald the opportunity to learn new skills from a helpful teacher, particularly in the areas of science or medicine. This is also a promising card for those with ambitions in the area of the performing arts, as it indicates new inspiration and exceptional talent.

Spiritually, the Druid is a card that indicates divine inspiration. You are being called on to explore your own spiritual heritage, which is bound up with the land you live in and the earth you walk on—the old ways lost from the sight of humankind and kept in secret by the spirits of ancient forests, sacred wells and springs, buried in the earth, blown on the wind, and carried by the trees, herbs, and animals. These are the energies that come directly from the primal source of the Divine, pure and unsullied by the dogmas, misrepresentations, and misunderstandings of humankind.

Reverse Meanings

The Druid reversed always indicates an imbalance of some kind, whether it is one of approach, attitude, or lifestyle. Your attitudes are rather rigid and set; you don't even like to think about things that don't fall into the pattern you have tried to impose on life. Anything new is rather frightening and you feel safer sticking to established forms. Remember that you need to achieve a balance in life—time to work, time to play, time to be busy, time to rest, time you give to others, time you give to yourself. You need to look after your material concerns in the world and also the well-being of your mind and spirit. You must also leave space in your life for new and beautiful experiences to come to you.

Beware of taking advice from a man, it will not help, and he is possibly misrepresenting the situation for his own ulterior motives.

The Journey of the Fool

The fool has encountered the male and female aspects of himself and the male and female aspects of nature. He has been made aware of his intellect and his intuition, his physical body, and his spirit. He has learned that he lives in a world of opposites—day and night, summer and winter, male and female, body and spirit. Now, from the Druid, he learns that these opposites must be balanced in his life. He is neither a purely spiritual being nor purely a material one, and this duality is part of being human. His job now is to accept and harmonize these aspects within himself and without.

The Lovers

The card shows the May King and Queen about to undergo their ritual marriage. They dance around a maypole of birch wood. The Queen wears a garland of flowers and the King is clad in green. In the background is a hawthorn tree in full blossom, and in the foreground a cuckoo pint. A dove circles the sky above the maypole.

The Symbolism

The rising of the Pleiades and the flowering of the hawthorn in May signals the start of the fire festival of Beltane—which means "bright-fire"—a May celebration of life and fertility. The weather is getting warmer, the seeds have been planted, and the young animals have been born. We rejoice in the change of weather and energy. At Beltane, the Lord and Lady approach their sacred marriage, which gives life to the earth.

In folk custom, the election of the May King and Queen still happens in many parts of the country. She is covered in flowers, while he is covered in ivy, holly, birch, poplar, and fir greenery. In ancient times, they would have been the priest-king, the incarnation of the resurgent vegetation spirit, and the priestess, representing the Goddess. Their ritual marriage magically assisted fertility and growth and a good performance reflected on the well-being of the community. In some places, the May King and Queen are still called the bride and groom.

The population at large would also indulge in a certain amount of sexual license to ensure the fertility of the land by sympathetic magic. Any children of these "greenwood marriages" would be named sons of the God, hence surnames like Robins-son and Hods-son. Such entertaining practices were hard to stamp out and persisted well into the Middle Ages.

An ancient May Day practice that survives in popular culture is the maypole, a phallic symbol of fertility and revelry. Throughout Europe there are long traditions of a stripped tree of birch (for purification and the new season) or fir erected in the village square or sacred site and decorated with ribbons and greenery. The maypole or staff thrust into the earth, cave, or sacred well represented the fertilizing power of the God. Wells and other openings in the earth were considered to be entrances to the Underworld womb of the Goddess. The dance around the maypole, with some dancers circling sunwise, some widdershins, is a dance of death and rebirth. The tree represented the vegetation spirit, and people and houses were decked with greenery, and so came under the protection of the Green Spirit.

The taboo on bringing the sacred hawthorn indoors is lifted at Beltane. It is said that the scent of the hawthorn is reminiscent of female sexuality, the sexual flowering of the Goddess and the year. In medieval England, May Day was celebrated by riding out into the greenwood to collect greenery and may blossoms.

The Pleiades, in the constellation of Taurus, were also known as "the Doves," and the rising of these stars is one of the markers of the Beltane festival. As they pair for life, doves are the emblem of faithfulness. Magically, the dove represents the spirit of light and the soul. Doves were also associated with mother goddesses, symbolizing the soul or breath that is derived from the Mother.

Divinatory Meanings

The card of the Lovers shows the union of opposites to make a single whole greater than the sum of its parts.

When the Lovers card appears in your spread, it always indicates a difficult choice, usually in matters of love, but depending on surrounding cards it can be a choice concerning your career, family, or property. Every choice you make has consequences that can be far-reaching. Through your choices you determine the course of your life, and you must accept responsibility for what you have chosen. The choice of a partner is probably most important of all and will affect every area of your life. The card counsels you not to be hasty and rush into a relationship or marriage before you have thought it through. The immediate gratification of desire is tempting, but what will the long-term consequences be? It is no good trying to blame other people at a later date for a course of action you have chosen.

On a deeper level, it is time to learn that you are responsible for your own fate through the choices you have made. The results of these choices may be happy or painful, but it is through acknowledging the consequences of your actions that you gain experience and self-knowledge. The choices you make now will determine your future.

Spiritually, this card is a messenger of the higher realms, telling you of the importance of truth and the purest of motives.

Reverse Meanings

The Lovers reversed indicates that you are refusing to take responsibility for the consequences of your own actions. You made a hasty choice based purely on the desire for instant gratification and you are now trying to lay the blame on others or on fate. The Lovers reversed usually indicates a love triangle.

In some circumstances, the Lovers reversed can indicate inner conflicts, being at war with yourself rather than external forces. Perhaps you are punishing yourself for something you have done or feel responsible for? This is not helping you or anyone else. You must do what you can to make amends, and if this is not possible, let the past go and resolve to make better choices in the future.

The Journey of the Fool

In card five, the Druid, the fool learned about balancing opposites and polarities. In this card, the Lovers, he learns about the marriage and fusion of those opposites to make a single whole. He now connects with the Divine Spirit and becomes aware of the transcendence of the spirit and the development of the eternal soul through the choices he makes.

The Chariot

The card shows Boudicca, the warrior queen of the Iceni in her war chariot, drawn by two horses—one black, one white. Her face is stained with woad, painted in spiral patterns. She brandishes a whip.

The Symbolism

The warrior queen of the Iceni, Boudicca led her tribe against the Romans. Here, in her war chariot, she is urging the two horses to greater efforts by brandishing her whip.

The Iceni took their name from the horse. Horses represent the land itself, virility, fertility, strength, and swiftness, as well as being the steeds of sun and moon deities. Horse cults existed in Britain long before the coming of the Celts. The horse was a favorite tribal totem or god of the Iron and Bronze Ages and was depicted on the earliest Celtic coins.

White horses symbolize the sun and the light half of the year, while black horses are connected with the dark half of the year, death, and the Underworld. These ancient mythological connections survive to this day in folklore ceremonies, such as the midwinter horsing ceremonies, which often involve a death and resurrection mumming play and the appearance of the Hobby Horses of Padstow and Minehead at Beltane. The sinister black Padstow *'obby 'oss* parades through the town accompanied by a teaser who leads him on. At times the music falls silent and the 'oss gradually falls to the floor, only to rise again, though at midnight he dies, to be born again the next summer.

The black horse was considered unlucky, funerary, heralding death, and symbolizing chaos. It was said to appear during the twelve days of chaos between the old and new year at midwinter. White animals were generally associated with sky deities, black animals with Underworld deities. The Celts believed that souls traveled to the land of the dead on horseback.

The Celtic horse and hound god was Fal, a god of light amid darkness. The northern quarter was known as "the Plain of Fal"— truth and wisdom, containing the Stone of Fal, the station of the circle associated with the winter solstice and the rebirth of the midwinter sun. Significantly, in Celtic myth the horse goddess Rhiannon gives birth to her son at the midwinter solstice.

In this card, the horses represent the animal, instinctive side of human nature. Some characteristics of this side of ourselves, such as aggression, have to be tamed and controlled. The driver of the chariot represents the intellect, which controls these potentially destructive instincts with the help of bit and bridle. The bit and bridle betoken control, endurance, and temperance. The horses symbolize the physical life-force, while the reins are will and intelligence.

Divinatory Meanings

The horses harnessed to the chariot are controlled by the driver, representing the control of instincts and impulses by willpower and self-discipline. This is not to say that instinctive primal impulse and raw talent should be suppressed, rather it is a matter of achieving the difficult balance of channeling them into achieving something useful without destroying them.

If the card of the chariot appears in your spread, it indicates that you will have to use the strength of your will to overcome obstacles. You need to be determined, self-disciplined, and hard working. If you are, you will triumph over any difficulties or any people who are trying to limit you. This struggle will ultimately temper you and make you stronger. This is an important card for disabled people, advising that a very successful life can be built up within the limitations that have been put on you; you only have to want it enough.

On a deeper level, the chariot is telling you that you must come to terms with your own aggressive impulses. Aggression is part of human nature, part of your innate survival mechanism. Aggression cannot be simply suppressed; to do so will only turn it inward on yourself, leaving it thereafter to manifest in the form of physical illness. Aggression can be very destructive, but it is also a powerful energy that can be channeled creatively.

Reverse Meanings

You are collapsing under pressure and losing your self-control. Your aggression is being channeled in the wrong direction—wildly at other people, at fate, at circumstances. This is a complete waste of your energy and resources. Redefine your aggression as determination and willpower, stop clinging weakly to unrewarding ideas, habits, people, and objects and move forward.

The Journey of the Fool

In the previous card, the Fool met the Lovers and was given a spiritual vision. However, he now learns that this is not enough, he must make his way through the world while he sustains this vision. He realizes that while he needs willpower and courage, these qualities are reflected in darker measures in his personality. Only by accepting them as part of the whole can he move forward.

The Warrior

The card shows the British warrior woman Scathach, who trained the Irish hero Cuchulain in her school for warriors. Her name means "the Shadowy One." She readies herself for the Lughnasa games to prove her worth. A borage plant grows at her feet and she is accompanied by her familiar, the badger.

The Symbolism

This card depicts a warrior whose strengths and skills have been honed through practice and trial. The warrior is self-confident and radiates an inner strength that stems from the knowledge that she has the experience and ability to deal with whatever she may face.

The Warrior's familiar is the badger, one of the strongest woodland animals. Even when set upon by several dogs, it can hold its own. Badger is close to the earth and dwells within it, making elaborate setts underground. One of the lessons of the badger is how to maintain your integrity and strength when everything around you seems set on pulling you down and the opposition is overwhelming. Badger draws his power from his closeness to the earth. Badger also knows the secrets that reside within the earth, digging and delving into his underground home. He knows the importance of a retreat within.

The badger is a powerful familiar. He is an ancient dweller of Albion and knows all its secrets—the sacred places of the land and the energies of all of them. He understands the power of all that grows within the earth. Badger is a warrior and it is the Warrior's Path he teaches. His weapons are his own body, his mind, and his spirit. The Will of the badger is centered, grounded, and unshakable. His courage is indomitable.

Borage was one of the magical herbs of the Celts. The common name is from the Celtic word *borrach* meaning "person of strong courage or bravery." Our Celtic ancestors would steep borage leaves in wine; the mixture resulted in a very significant rise in the blood adrenaline level. To give courage to the Crusaders, borage was added to the stirrup cups drunk at their departure. We use borage to stimulate courage and strength—it is particularly useful when exploring the warrior path and the male aspects of your own personality.

Divinatory Meanings

The warrior here is a psychic warrior, with body, mind, and spirit as weapons. These must be trained to work in harmony. The warrior faces her own fears, develops her spiritual courage and hones the Will. Will is not impulse or desire, or even willpower as in the card of the Chariot. It is the unwavering strength that seeks the personal truth and path.

If the card of the Warrior appears in your spread, it shows that you will have the opportunity to put plans into action. It is a card of powerful forward-moving energies, indicating that you can master adverse circumstances through your determination and courage. However, while you must be firm, you must not be aggressive or lose your temper—this behavior will make you lose ground. Whatever your fight, you must keep a clear head and a calm demeanor—and remember to be magnanimous in victory.

Spiritually, this card speaks about the development of the Will. The warrior may subject herself to physical extremes to force her will and consciousness beyond the ordinary. We are all subject to many fears, and it is the warrior's purpose to seek them out and defeat them. It must be recognized that the body has its own fears—fear of injury, fear of physical danger—which are natural and proper. Without these fears, we would put our hands in the fire, crash our cars, or jump off cliffs. The body has an innate mechanism of self-preservation. It clings to life, that's its job. The warrior may decide to face many physical fears to develop Will and courage—fear facilitates a change in consciousness; to conquer a fear facilitates the development of the Will. To do something so dangerous that it may result in injury or death, however, is no part of the warrior's path, it is a self-indulgence. The deepest fears lie within the mind itself, they arise from childhood and adult experiences and conditioning. Such fears limit us, and prevent our development. At some point, the warrior must confront them, one by one, and deal with them. Your spirituality is your own quest, and you must find your own truth. You can, however, test and push yourself, run that extra mile, swim the extra two lengths, dig the extra few yards. You can do much more than you imagine— break your self-imposed limits.

Reverse Meanings

The opposite to the spirit of the warrior is the childish response of rage and tantrums to situations where you don't get your own way. If this card appears reversed in your spread it means that you do not yet have the spirit of the warrior, you want always to be the center of attention and you sulk or react angrily and destructively when you are not.

The self-respect of the warrior is won through trial and experience. It is never boasted about or used to inflate one's ego. The warrior has personal integrity and treats others with equal consideration. The warrior is at peace with herself, her strength does not come from building a hard shell around herself that contains and suppresses all feelings and passions. If this is what you have done, you are called on to recognize that this is a weakness, not a strength, arising from a fear of letting other people know the real you, thus giving them the imagined power to hurt you. The warrior has conquered these fears and cannot be hurt in this way.

You must go within yourself and find your own strength. If you feel powerless and angry, stop blaming other people, they can only do to you what you allow them to, they can only make you feel what you allow them to. Take back your personal power and the control of your own life. Use your energies to construct what you want for yourself, don't waste them on blame and regret.

Like the badger, you should look into the power of the earth. Magically, spiritually, or emotionally, you may be ungrounded and dissipating your energies. Contact the earth, feel its power and ability to sustain. See the herbs and roots it provides to heal the body and the soul.

The Journey of the Fool

At this point, the fool discovers that he must begin to develop his spiritual Will as opposed to desire or even the determination and willpower of the Chariot. This involves going deep inside himself to develop his strength by confronting the fears that lie within, and by following his path boldly, wherever it leads.

The Shaman

The card shows a Celtic shaman clad in deerskin. He lives alone in the forest with only his animal familiar, the wolf, for company. He sits before his cauldron, in which he is boiling a brew of inspiration that will enable him to travel to the spirit world. Some of the ingredients lie on the ground, including the sacred vervain herb. Beating his *bodhran*, he calls to the spirits.

The Symbolism

Central to the Celtic shaman's path is a relationship with the land—in a real, not symbolic, manner. He observes and celebrates the wheel of the seasons and becomes part of their ebb and flow. He seeks to personally encounter and connect with the spirits of the land to gain their teachings and to honor them.

His quest is the transformation of himself by virtue of a constantly expanding state of consciousness, an awareness of the subtle workings of the universe. He has committed himself to a continuous journey of discovery. He seeks not to walk the path but to become the path.

To the shaman, everything possesses spirit, a living force within it that vibrates to the pulse of the earth. It is the Divine energy of the Goddess and the God that permeates everything—people, animals, plants, rocks, the land itself. He recognizes and works with this force, knowing that because this force is Divine, all things that contain it are sacred; manifest Nature is sacred and connects all things within it. Through this power he mediates between the world of spirits and the world of humankind.

Celtic shamans sought an expansion of consciousness through a magical drink known as the Cauldron of Ceridwen, which bestowed the powers of eloquence, inspiration, prophecy, and song. It contained "the ruddy gem" of rowan; the foam of the ocean, Taliesin's cresses; Gwion's silver, the flixweed; and vervain kept apart from the influence of the moon. A part of this potion was also added to the *Gwin* or *Bragwod*, the sacred drink of British initiates made of wine, water, barley, and meal. In one sense, this drink was a real brew, in another it represented the process of knowledge.

In legend, the goddess Ceridwen brewed a potion that contained all the wisdom of the Three Realms. The herbs were ritually collected and the cauldron brewed for a year and a day. A little boy, Gwion, was given the job of feeding the fire beneath it. One day, three drops fell from the cauldron onto his finger, which he put into his mouth to ease the pain. Instantly he was at one with all things past, present, and future. The knowledge then made him afraid and he tried to run away from it. The Goddess challenged him by assuming a frightening form to test his worthiness. Gwion fled from her by assuming different personifications of animal familiars, assimilating the knowledge of different realities. The Goddess herself shapeshifted into different forms to pursue him, forcing him on to new realities, refining his being. Eventually he assumed the shape of a grain of wheat, which the Goddess, in the form of a black hen, ate. In other words, he had to be reassumed into the womb of the Goddess in order to be reborn as a true initiate. The womb of the Underworld Goddess contains both the seeds of new growth and the souls of the dead. Nine months later he was reborn as Taliesin, which means "radiant brow."

One of the main ingredients of the Cauldron of Ceridwen was vervain. One of the three most sacred herbs of the Druids, it was gathered only at the rising of the Dog Star, Sirius, when neither the sun nor the moon cast a light. Vervain is used at Samhain, the festival that celebrates the two aspects of the womb of the Goddess, the seed that lies within it dormant until the spring, and the souls of the ancestors who are called upon to share their wisdom.

The Celtic shaman of the card is shown with his familiar, the wolf. In European lore, the wolf is regarded with awe. Wolves were thought to be very wise and, if they chose to, could share their knowledge with people. In one tale, the druid Bobaran met the white wolf Emhain Abhlac. He threw three rowan berries into the air, three at the wolf, and three into his own mouth to receive the insight of the wolf. Merlin is said to have retired into the woodlands for several years and took as his companion a very old wolf. Cernunnos is depicted with a wolf on the Gundestrup cauldron. The goddess Brighid also is depicted with a wolf; it is one of her four sacred animals and one of the totem guardians of Britain.

In Celtic lore, the wolf rules over the winter quarter of purification and death from Samhain to Imbolc—the dead time of the year when the earth sleeps, making itself ready to regenerate in the spring. February was called *Faoilleach*, which means "the wolf month" or "the storm month/month of bleak death," during which the festival of Imbolc, the feast of the goddess Brighid, fell.

The shaman's wolf familiar teaches him the development of his instincts and his psychic side under the auspices of the moon. Wolf is a guide to new knowledge, the kind that is gained by learning to trust yourself and your own inner voice. Wolf is teaching the shaman to go deep within himself for the answers.

Divinatory Meanings

We are accustomed to experiencing the world through our five senses and the interpretation of the information derived from them. Our responses are based on them, and by our memory and experiences that keep the shape of the world as it superficially appears. The shaman learns to expand his consciousness and understanding to take into account other, more subtle, realms. From childhood, we are taught to suppress this ability—our instincts, intuition, clairvoyance. The shaman is learning to recover his other senses, to unlearn thought structures that have been instilled as he developed, the constant mental reinforcement of his existing perceptions of the world that prevent other levels of consciousness becoming apparent.

When the Shaman card appears in your spread, it indicates a time to show prudence. You should stand back from current events and not participate in them. Keep a distance so that you can make a clearer evaluation of what is going on. This is a time for careful planning, not action.

On a deeper level, this card indicates that this is a time of withdrawal for you, a necessary period of isolation when you can come to know yourself better and learn to rely on yourself rather than others.

Spiritually, this is a very important card indicating that you will receive illumination from within.

Reverse Meanings

This reversed card indicates suspicion of others' motives that is groundless, a stubborn clinging to bad habits and lifestyles, or jumping in without thought. It is a card of shallow knowledge, of reliance on what you are told, rather than what you have experienced yourself.

The Journey of The Fool

This card is usually called The Hermit, from a Greek word meaning *wilderness*. Here the Fool returns to the place where it all began, to commune with the spirits of nature. He has been taught many lessons by human advisors and has been given plenty of advice. Now he feels the need to be alone with nature to get to the source of things and to cut out the conflicting and clamorous voices of the world of humankind.

After a period of shaking off his conditioning, he prepares to take the initiatory drink, which is a symbol of the initial initiatory experience. The true initiation begins with a long search for knowledge and many years of study. Then, when the neophyte least expects it, will come an overwhelming vision of wonderful proportions. This will often leave the candidate with a feeling of harmony, belonging, and inviolability that will last for days or weeks. However, this is only the start of the process and there is no turning back. The Fool must move on from this card to confront the shadows of the Self, which he will experience as a series of journeys into the Underworld, learning and battling with the monsters of the Id.

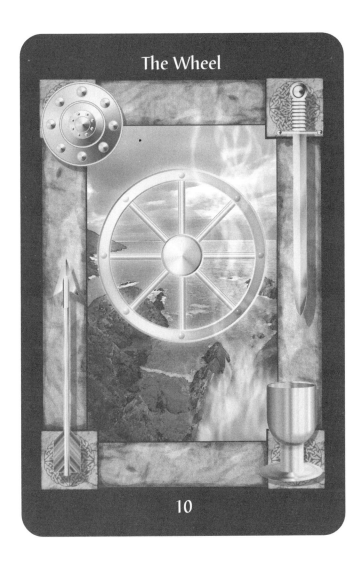

The Wheel

This card depicts the turning wheel, which symbolizes the passage of time and the cosmic forces of change. The four directions and the four elements are depicted with their corresponding four magical tools. The eight spokes represent the eight major festivals of the solar year.

The Symbolism

The turning of the circle or wheel indicates spinning through time and the seasons. The sun, which appears to us as a circular disc, passes through each house of the zodiac during the year, strengthening and weakening as it goes. The eight festivals that divide the year are the spokes of the wheel when energy enters or leaves the earth. Within the year is an ebb and flow reflecting the passage of the seasons. The Craft year reflects the tide of Nature. Each festival is a celebration. The four solar festivals may be seen as aligning with the cardinal points of the circle, and the four fire festivals with the cross-quarter points.

> **Samhain:** the start of winter, festival of the dead, around October 31
>
> **Yule:** the winter solstice, the rebirth of the sun, around December 21
>
> **Imbolc:** the first stirrings of spring, the coming of the Maiden Goddess, around February 2
>
> **Ostara:** the vernal equinox, celebration of spring and the growing light, around March 21
>
> **Beltane:** the sacred marriage of the Lord and Lady, the start of summer and fertility around May 1
>
> **Coamhain:** the summer solstice, the zenith of the sun and summer around June 21
>
> **Lughnasa:** the beginning of the harvest, the prime of the Corn Lord, around August 2
>
> **Herfest:** the autumn equinox, the harvest festival, death of the Corn Lord, waning of the sun, around September 21

The four cardinal points of the circle mark the seasons of the sun and are associated with the four elements. These are not elements as one thinks of chemical elements on the periodic table. They are the basic powers of things on both the material and astral plane, not their chemical composition. Like the cardinal quarters, the elements also embody certain ideas and qualities.

The north is the point of the circle associated with the winter solstice (Yule), cold, darkness, starlight, old age, and death. However, it is also the point of regeneration and rebirth, life through death, as it is at the winter solstice that the sun is reborn. It then gains strength and grows stronger until the summer solstice. North is associated with the element of earth. For the Celts, the mystical north was represented by the city or castle of Falias. This refers to the element of earth, not the planet. Earth is solid, like the bones that structure our bodies. Rocks, stones, and crystals are often seen as the bones of Mother Earth, Herself. Earth is the densest of all the elements. It is associated with the perceptions of our five ordinary senses—seeing, hearing, smelling, tasting, and touching. From the stuff of the earth grow all living things, its immense nurturing power can sustain the greatest oak tree and the tiniest flower. It is symbolized by the pentacle, the shield, the stone, or the disc suit of the tarot.

The east is the point of the circle associated with the spring equinox (Ostara). The sun rises in the east, it is sunrise and gestation, the beginning of growth, a time of green youth. It is associated with the element of air. In a stone circle oriented to the vernal equinox, the sun will rise directly in the east, over the east stone at the equinox. For the Celts, the mystical east was represented by the city or castle of Gorias. Air is a gas: invisible, it is felt only in the wind. Air is the breath that sustains us, the rhythm and energy of life itself. It is associated with thought and the powers of the mind. It is represented by the sword, the athame, and the sword suit of the tarot.

The south is the point of the circle associated with the summer solstice (Coamhain), with the zenith of the sun's strength, with things beginning to ripen, and with maturity and the prime of life. It is associated with the element of fire. For the Celts, the south was represented by the city or castle of Finias. Fire seems the most mysterious of all the elements. It transforms that which it consumes. It is associated with the spirit and with intuition. It is represented by the wand, the staff, the rod, the arrow, the spear, and the wand suit of the tarot.

The west is the point of the circle associated with the autumn equinox—Herfest—and the completion of the harvest, as well as with twilight, completion, and decline. It is associated with the element of water. For the Celts, the mystical west was represented by the city or castle of Murias. Water is liquid, like the blood that flows through our veins. All life started in the rich biological soup of the oceans, just as you were protected by the uterine waters of your mother's womb. It is associated with emotions, feelings, and the subconscious mind. It is represented by the chalice, the cauldron, the well, the spring, and the cup suit of the tarot.

The four streams of elemental energy—the four Royal Roads of Power—coming from the cardinal points meet at the center of the circle. This point becomes the *axis mundi*, the center of all things where all times and places are one, from which all things are accessible. It may be symbolized by the pillar, the shaman's ladder, the world tree, or the cauldron of renewal. For the Celts, it was the Spiral or the Glass Castle, a place of regeneration and rebirth, the axis through the center linking all realms and times. The center is the place of initiation and rebirth. The spiral or maze dance within the circle moves inwards representing death, to the center point of renewal, and outward again in rebirth.

Divinatory Meanings

This card is often called Fortune, indicating that all things are transient and change at the whim of fate. It might more properly be called "karma" as it shows the turning of the wheel—what has been sown shall be reaped in its season. It sometimes seems that some people are blessed with good luck while others are cursed with ill, but in reality you sow the seeds of your own fate with your actions or inaction, your words or silence, or your attitudes. The appearance of this card in a spread indicates that the wind of change is blowing, but the seeming sudden changes that occur come as the results of past efforts—whether for good or ill— though they will lead to a new phase in your life when you will grow enormously.

The Wheel calls upon you to be sensitive to the ebb and flow of the cycles surrounding you: when to act, when to be still; when to talk, when to listen; when to hold on and when to let go. Things don't always happen when we want them to, but instead when it is their season. No farmer needs a calendar to tell him when to plant or reap; sheep don't look at calendars to tell them when to lamb. The old countryman planned his year by observation of the sun, moon, and stars, the changes in the weather, the development of plant and animal life. For our ancestors, Beltane, Lughnasa, Imbolc, and Samhain were not celebrated on particular dates, but when the "time was right."

Reverse Meanings

The Wheel reversed indicates that you are resisting a change that is inevitable. What does not change stagnates, and it is impossible that things should always remain the same. All things are born and grow, then wither and die. This is the only certainty and it is not a bleak one—from death comes rebirth. One thing must end for another to begin. To welcome change is a liberating experience.

The Journey of the Fool

In the journey of spiritual evolution, which the tarot describes, the Wheel represents the seeker's dawning awareness of the cosmic forces that turn the wheel, the energies of the four elements. The first resonance of the elements is in your own body—earth as bone, air as breath, water as blood, and fire as spirit. The elements flow through the universe, consolidating, dissolving, transforming, a flow of energy that shapes and changes all things in a never ending cycle. The elements represent different levels of consciousness but they must always be in balance, they are interdependent.

The Web

This shows the Weaver Goddess standing in an autumnal clearing. She is dressed in brown and gold robes and carries a knife. At her side is a white dog with red ears. At the corners of the card are juniper berries, hazel nuts, and a spider within a web.

The Symbolism

In Welsh legend, the Weaver Goddess is Arianrhod, mistress of Caer Arianrhod, the Spiral Castle of death, initiation, and rebirth. Out of her own body she spins the thread of being and weaves it to form matter—the cosmos itself. She is the Goddess of Fate who spins the thread of destiny and weaves the web that joins all life together. Her spinning wheel is the wheel of the stars, her threads the threads of life, death, and rebirth. Her castle reflects the spiralling thread. The ancients saw it as the Corona Borealis at the North Star, where souls regenerated. The spiral shape, which is the basis of the spider's web, is an ancient and nearly universal symbol of regeneration and rebirth. It is the spiral maze of life and death.

All things contain spirit or life-force, whether they are human, animal, plant, or stone, which vibrates to the pulse of the earth itself. This life-force is linked together in a web of being, a net of power that joins and gives life to the cosmos. As Pagans, this is the force that we work with, and through this web we mediate between the world of spirits and the world of humankind. The magician can integrate with and communicate with the web, and through its fibers, perform magic. As our understanding and consciousness grows, we become aware of the working of the web and its more subtle realms. We are part of the web, we can attune to its various energies and magically vibrate the web with full knowledge of the outcome. Any vibration on the web eventually reverberates everywhere else, like ripples moving out from a stone thrown into a pond.

The symbol of the Weaver Goddess is the spider, the archetypal spinner and weaver, and its web pattern was discerned as the pattern of life itself. It is sacred to all spinning and weaving goddesses, and the goddesses of fate. Some say that the spider's web is the thirteenth sign of the zodiac, representing fate and destiny. Spider patiently spins her web with the skill of a craftsman, sometimes trying again and again until she has got it right. She teaches the ways and patterns of the web. Spider teaches how to magically vibrate the web to cause the desired effect and the extent of that effect. Spider knows how things travel the web and what they mean. Spiders have eight legs, representing the four winds and the four directions, and the eight festivals—eight is the number of solar increase and the symbol of infinity.

The Goddess weaves the thread of a person's fate according to their actions within the web of life. As such, she can be seen as the Goddess of Justice, ready to change the pattern of the weave or, with her knife, to cut the thread. She is shown with her plant familiars, the hazel and the juniper.

In ogham the hazel is *coll*, one of the seven chieftain trees. It is a symbol of wisdom that can be used to create or destroy. The ancient "dripping hazel" is an example of the symbol of wisdom put to destructive use. It was a leafless tree that was home to ravens and vultures; the sap that it dripped was poisonous. When the hero Fionn used its wood for a battle shield, it gave off fumes that killed thousands.

The juniper is a tree of purification, and in European lore it is associated with goddesses of justice and truth. It is also sacred to the spirits of divine vengeance sent by the gods to administer justice.

The Goddess of Justice's animal familiar is the fairy hunting dog. These otherworldy animals have white bodies and red ears and are called the Cwn Annwn, or Underworld hounds. Many legends of Britain tell of the Wild Hunt, a pack of ghostly dogs who fly through the night sky to pursue their quarry of evildoers. The prey is variously described in legend as a white stag or a white boar—both soul animals—or as the souls of the damned. Skilled magicians have, at times, invoked the power of the Wild Hunt to chase down those who have committed great evils, though great care has to be taken. If the cause is unjust, the Hunt will carry off their invoker.

Divinatory Meanings

The Web card relates to your sense of Self, the realization of yourself as an individual, but as an individual who is nevertheless connected with the planet you live on and the other life that inhabits it. It relates to the development of a personal morality and conscience, an inner sense of right and wrong. You must recognize that your actions and words do not exist in isolation, but also affect others. Being polite and charming because you want people to like you is not enough, you must deal with people fairly and sensitively because those qualities are meaningful and important to you.

It is the card of the Weaver Goddess, who spins the thread of life and the pattern of fate. Her web connects all things in a net of power, and your actions vibrate the web, affecting all that lies along the thread. Through the web, every action will eventually return to you. This is what is meant by the Pagan Law of Threefold Return—your actions will return to you threefold, amplified by the web, whether they are actions for good or ill. In other words, you construct your own fate and are the instrument of your own justice.

When the Web card appears in your spread, it is telling you that you must make a decision based on your own sense of what is right rather than listening to the advice of others. Any action you take must be based on careful deliberation considering its far-reaching effects on yourself and others. Depending on surrounding cards, the Web card can indicate that truth and justice will prevail in a dispute, perhaps even a legal action.

Reverse Meanings

The Web card reversed can indicate that you may be the victim of some injustice, being falsely accused of some action or misrepresented by gossips. Someone may be unreasonably biased against you and you may be passed over for promotion. However, you must ask yourself why this should be—have you always dealt fairly and considerately with the people involved? Or have you been indulging in gossip, yourself? Nothing happens in isolation or without any cause whatsoever, though you may have to dig deep to find it. Legal actions will be delayed and complications may arise.

The Journey of the Fool

Here the Fool encounters the Web, the invisible thread that links all life in the cosmos. He realizes that he does not exist or act in isolation, and that on every level he interacts with and affects everything and everyone he comes into contact with. His actions do not only have consequences for himself, but for other people, other creatures, the environment, and the planet. He realizes that his past actions have created his present, and present actions will create his future and affect the future of others through the workings of the web in both an obvious and a subtle way. Up until this point he has only been concerned with himself, his own consciousness and his relationship with Nature. Now he must consider the far-reaching consequences of his relationships and actions.

Sacrifice

The card shows the man of corn or corn dolly, which represents the sacrificed life of the corn spirit so that humankind might eat. Illustrated in the border of the card are poppies, cornflowers, blackberries, and a harvest mouse.

The Symbolism

The gathering of the harvest is still a time fraught with anxiety. Will the weather hold? Will the harvest be good? It is, after all, the culmination of the year's work on the farm. In former times, the whole community would take part in the harvest. The cutting of the final sheaf was particularly dangerous because it contained the life spirit of the corn, which had retreated into the final stook. Sometimes the harvesters would approach it reverently, calling it "the neck," or sometimes "the mare," and cut it in a single stroke with the cry "I have the neck." This was then carefully woven into a corn-dolly or kern-baby, which would preserve the corn spirit safely until the next year. It would be kept in a place of honor until the spring, when it would be plowed into the fields to bring them life. The shapes of the corn dolly are traditional to different areas, such as the Durham chandelier, the Northamptonshire horns, and the Suffolk horseshoe. The ribbons that bind it are significant in their colors—yellow for the sun, red for sacrifice, blue for love, green for wisdom, and white for strength. The sacrifice of the corn spirit is necessary in order that humankind has enough food to eat for the coming year.

The blood-red poppies appearing in the corn fields at harvest time represent the fruit of the Underworld womb of the Harvest Mother, while the white poppy juice is as the nourishing milk from her breasts. The generic name *papaver* is thought to come from the Latin *pappa*, which means *a breast*. In the ancient world, it was believed that the quality of the corn would be improved by the presence of poppies in the fields. They were offered, together with some symbolic corn, to the Harvest Goddess. The flowers symbolize fertility, plenty, and abundance, as well as sacrifice.

The cornflower, like the field poppy, represents the gifts of the Harvest Mother, who brings forth life from her womb, but who also slays the Corn Lord. At Herfest, the invoking priest and priestess wear garlands of cornflowers, and the petals are added to incenses and the ritual cup.

The bramble was a sacred plant of the Celts. In Scotland, the bramble, along with the rowan and the yew, constituted the sacred fire. In ogham the blackberry is *muin*. A taboo on eating blackberries exists in Celtic countries—in Brittany and Cornwall the reason given is that the blackberry belongs to the fairy folk. The five-petaled flowers associate the blackberry very strongly with the Goddess, and the fruit, which appears green at first, then red, and finally black, represents the three stages of the Goddess and the completion of the cycle. Blackberries provide the wine at the autumn equinox, which marks the end of the harvest and the completion of the cycle. The Harvest Lord enters the Underworld at Herfest, the realm of the Sidhe—the fairy folk, the People of the Mounds—and is given into their care.

Mice were regarded as Underworld animals because of their habit of living underground and in dark places. They could travel between the world of men and the Underworld along secret paths, getting through the tiniest crack to escape danger. Mice were soul animals, and legends tell of people whose souls, shaped like mice, came out of their mouths while they slept.

Divinatory Meanings

It is the law of Nature that one thing must die for another to live. To eat we must take the lives of plants and animals, or their potential lives in seeds, fruits, and eggs. The ancient people reverenced these lives as they were taken, appreciated, and made ritual restitution for the sacrifice made. For farming communities the autumn harvest was the culmination of the work of the year, but involved the sacrifice of the vegetation spirit, which had returned with the spring to thrive with the summer—a sacrifice necessary for the greater good.

When this card appears in your spread, it indicates that a willing sacrifice of some kind will be called for. You will be forced to recognize the necessity of change, which involves letting one thing go to gain another, whether this concerns relationships, possessions, or personal growth. Depending on the surrounding cards, it may be that the time has come to relinquish a long-cherished dream or ambition that cannot be fulfilled, but which is standing in the way of you pursuing another, and ultimately more beneficial, course. It may be that you decide to shed the burdens of social position, business, or possessions to achieve an inner peace.

On a deeper level, the Sacrifice card is asking you to look at your attitudes toward control. It may be that you feel the need to keep tight control on every area of your life—your possessions, your emotions, your relationships, and your attitudes. Loss of control is very frightening to you, and this fear is preventing your growth. You are missing out on the excitement of the unknown and the opportunity to discover new things and new experiences. Sometimes it is necessary to relax and let go, to let events take their course.

Reverse Meanings

If the Sacrifice card appears reversed in your spread, it indicates that you have become obsessed with control. You are letting many opportunities pass you by for fear of losing those things you already have, whether they are useful to you or not. You may be storing a lot of useless junk, in all senses, because you are loath to let anything go. You may be trying to control the lives of your children or your friends to suit yourself, rather than in a true desire for the best for them. Real love is giving people the freedom to become themselves.

The mouse of this card is warning you that you are in danger of becoming obsessed with small details, with cataloging things and putting them in order, and missing out on the bigger picture. You can't see the wood for the trees. Mouse may be telling you that you are making something that is really very simple unnecessarily difficult. As a familiar, Mouse is a specialist, teaching you how to organize your knowledge. Bits and pieces of information may be interesting, but can also be misleading or dangerous taken out of context. Too many people are information butterflies, alighting first on one subject, then another, then another, briefly extracting an idea, a ritual. Though details may be fascinating, you also need to step back and look at the whole picture.

The Journey of the Fool

With this card, the Fool has come to a realization that he is on the verge of a greater consciousness that cannot be attained by the intellect or by physical action. He must surrender himself to the greater forces of the cosmos and let them do with him as they will. This involves the sacrifice of all that he has previously learned and held sacred, all of his shields and defenses, the things that he has felt have been giving him control over his life and destiny. He has made a blind leap into the dark, acting on faith alone, and hangs suspended between his old self and the new. He is alone, vulnerable and afraid, waiting for what will come.

Death

The card depicts the Harvest Goddess—the terrifying crone aspect of Ceridwen. Robed and hooded in purple, she wields a crescent-moon-shaped sickle, about to reap the last sheaf of corn. It is night and the full harvest moon rises in the sky. The border of the card is decorated with ivy, skulls, and corn.

The Symbolism

In this card, we encounter the Dark Goddess, the Crone or Cailleach. She is the Goddess of death, destruction, and winter. With the autumn equinox comes the completion of the harvest; the golden crops matured by the sun are cut down by the crescent-moon sickle, the talisman or symbol of the Death Goddess, with which she reaps the harvest of souls.

In Scotland, the last sheaf of corn was fashioned into the likeness of a woman and was called the Cailleach (old woman) or Famine of the Farm. The man who cut the last sheaf was called "Winter" and underwent various insults and had to look after the Cailleach all winter, a duty considered very unlucky as it meant probable death to the farmer, his family, or his stock. Attempts were often made to pass the Cailleach on to others who had not yet completed their harvests. The corn dolly was often called "the Corn Hag of Winter," as it withered and dried out.

The ivy is sometimes seen as the female companion to the corn, the Goddess slayer of the Corn Lord. In England, the last sheaf to be cut in the harvest was bound with ivy and called "the Ivy Girl." The farmer who was last in with his harvest was given the Ivy Girl as his penalty, and it represented bad luck until the following harvest. The Ivy Goddess is the force that slays the Corn Lord so that he may feed us all. But she takes him back into her womb to await rebirth, for her womb is the Underworld, where seeds germinate and souls await rebirth.

After the harvest, the year declines and the hours of daylight grow shorter. The next festival in the calendar is Samhain, the start of winter when the Dark Queen holds full sway and becomes the Samhain Mother who eats the souls of the dead, the White Sow aspect of Ceridwen, mistress of the Underworld whose womb swells with the souls of the dead. The winter half of the year is ruled by the Hag of Winter; she brings the cold and darkness, the vegetation dies down, and the earth sleeps.

It is no accident that the number of this Death card is thirteen. There are thirteen lunar months in a solar year, each lasting approximately twenty-eight days, stretching from full moon to full moon. Thirteen days after the waning of the full moon begins comes the time of the dark moon, or dead moon, when the moon is no longer visible in the sky. It was believed that the ancestors visited the earth from the moon by traveling along the beams into the long barrows where they could be contacted. The long barrows faced their entrances east so that they would be flooded with the light of the rising full moon. The Goddess was represented by the ancient people of this land as the burial mounds into which the dead were laid. These were both the tomb of the body and the earth womb of the Goddess where the soul awaits rebirth.

The Crone aspect of the Goddess is difficult to come to terms with. The Maiden in her beauty can be admired, as can the Mother in her fertility and sexuality. But is she admired as an old woman no longer fertile or desirable? This is perhaps one of the most important lessons of all. She is still feminine, still the Goddess. Hers is the wisdom, she is the Keeper of the Mysteries, the Dark Mother of the hidden, the darkness, the secrets of the tomb, and the guide to rebirth. She is Ceridwen, Morgan le Fey, Cale, the Cailleach, the Crone—the Goddess who shows the way to the expansion of levels of consciousness, she guards the gates of death and the Underworld and is the opener of the way. Ceridwen, the White Sow, is the British Underworld initiator who owns the cauldron of death and regeneration into which all souls are plunged at the ending of life.

The Goddess calls on us at this point in the cycle to enter the Underworld; her summer mother robes turn from purple to black. She is terrifying, a horror that we fear, but death comes to us all as a part of the cycle. To deny her is to deny half of ourselves. We try to flee from her mysteries, but hers is a beauty not given to those who do not look beyond the surface. Her dark cloak enfolds us in an ending of all desire, and we sleep in her care until another dawn.

Divinatory Meanings

This card does not presage a physical death but, like the harvest, marks the end of a cycle in which the seeds of a new one are sown. As the earth undergoes a yearly cycle of death and renewal, in our lives we undergo many such cycles.

The Death card marks the end of a phase of your life that can never be recaptured. This does not necessarily have unpleasant connotations—the birth of a child will mean a radical change of lifestyle, as might a marriage or a change of residence, but nevertheless the old way of life is dead and the loss must be acknowledged, come to terms with, and in some way mourned. The card indicates a time of such adjustment and mourning, a suspension between the old stage and the new.

Death always indicates a change, either voluntary or involuntary, good or bad. This change may come to you as a shock, it may be unexpected. Depending on surrounding cards, it can indicate an illness which will make you re-evaluate your life. Relationships may end, partnerships dissolve, jobs be lost, or businesses fail. Something must end—you can make this painful or easy, depending on whether you recognize the necessity of endings and change. If you can let go of the old life, an exciting new one can be just around the corner; try to hang onto the past, which is dead, and you will cause yourself pain.

On a higher level, the Death card can indicate that, because of experiences, all your pretensions are stripped away, leading to a re-evaluation of your life and a change in your consciousness—an ending that will lead you to a transformation.

Reverse Meanings

The Death card reversed indicates that you are refusing to accept change, you won't acknowledge that something has ended. If you don't release something voluntarily, it will cause you pain when it is snatched from you against your will. Refusal to change and grow beyond the dead past means stagnation and will lead to depression, boredom, and suffering.

The Journey of the Fool

The Goddess has led the fool to his death because only through his spiritual death can he be renewed and come to rebirth. She has asked him to sacrifice his image of himself to find his true Self; the old self must be left behind or "die" before a spiritual rebirth can take place. The frightening Cailleach is really the Wise Old Woman who guides him. She is the keeper of the mysteries.

Death has stripped the fool naked in order to go into the Underworld. He can take nothing with him, neither his old securities nor old beliefs.

The Underworld

The card shows King Gwyn ap Nudd in his Underworld domain of Annwn. He is robed in purple and wears a crown of lead and onyx. A white pig with red ears accompanies him. The border of the card shows two dragons—one red, one green—and branches of yew.

The Symbolism

The station of this card is Samhain, or Halloween, the start of winter and the Celtic New Year Festival. The Wheel of the Year is an eternal cycle of birth, growth, death, and rebirth. According to Celtic belief, before birth must come death—a natural and just part of the cycle. In all calculations of time night preceded day, thus Samhain Night, *oidhche Samhain*, was the night preceding Samhain, not the night after. To appreciate the full cycle of existence, decline and death must be accepted as natural events. These energies are recognized and respected at Samhain.

Samhain is the hinge of the year. For the Celts, any boundary was mystical. This could be a place between places, like the strand between sea and land; or a time between times, like dusk or dawn; or the witching hour of midnight, between one day and the next. Such times and places were treated with caution, as it was possible to pass through them to the Otherworld. The time when one season passed to another, such as Beltane and Samhain, were particularly tricky, because the Otherworld was very close—the veils between the realms were thin. Samhain is the pivotal point of the year itself, when one year passes to the next. The death spiral of the year is folding inward toward the point of renewal.

At Samhain, the gate to the Underworld stands open and the souls of the ancestors are sought for their guidance. The Underworld appears in many mythologies throughout the world. In modern times, it has come to be associated with the punishment of the Christian hell, but for the ancients it had no such connotations. It was the mysterious realm of the Dark Goddess and the Underworld Lord, the inner womb of the earth from which all life sprang and to which the spirit returned at death. There were various entrances to the Underworld in the physical realm such as caves, potholes, and wells through which heroes and visionaries might visit the Underworld in order to win its secrets. In psychological terms, the Underworld can be seen as the unconscious, the hidden inner self.

In the Death card we met the dark face of the Goddess. Here in the Underworld card we meet the darker face of the God. Here, after his death at Herfest, he reigns as Lord of the Dead, the protector of souls with whom he is forced to reside as he and they await rebirth.

He is shown accompanied by a fairy pig. According to the Welsh Mabinogion stories, the first pigs were a gift to Pryderi from the King of the Underworld. The sea god Manannan kept a magical herd of pigs in his Underworld kingdom; each animal killed and eaten at night would be reborn in the morning. Any human eating them would be made immortal. However, the water the pigs were cooked in would not boil until a truth was spoken for each quarter of the pig. Pig meat was once forbidden food in Celtic countries, just as it was in ancient Egypt and still is for Jewish people. Pigs were thought to be otherworldly creatures and their flesh formed the feasts of the Underworld, and was therefore taboo in the ordinary world. It could only safely be eaten by humankind once a year at a sacred feast at the winter solstice, the time of the rebirth of the sun as symbolized by Manannan's regenerating pigs.

The pig is sacred to the Lord of the Underworld and the Death Goddess. Orc is Irish for pig, hence the derivation of the name Orkneys, the island home of the Death Goddess. Pigs, with their crescent-shaped tusks, are associated with the moon. Their colors vary from white to red to black, the colors of the three phases of the moon. The white waxing phase relates to the virgin Goddess; the red full moon phase is the menstruating fertile Mother; the black waning phase is the Goddess of dissolution and death. Pigs feed on corpse flesh, are prolific breeders, and sometimes eat their own young—symbolizing the waning goddess of destruction. In several mythologies, it is a pig who devours the moon in its monthly cycles. One of the Goddess Ceridwen's aspects was as the Sow Goddess, "the old white one." Although she was mother and creatrix, like the sow that eats her own young, Ceridwen was the hag and devourer, who took the souls of her children back into her womb, the cauldron of inspiration and rebirth, to await another dawn.

Pig is a guide to Underworld knowledge. In Celtic myth, swineherds were honored as magicians and prophets. As a familiar, it teaches the ways of the Dark Goddess, the Hag of the Underworld whose frightening aspect is the initiatrix. Sow often begins the process of initiation, placing the candidate in the way of trials in the Underworld, forcing them to face the monsters of their own making: the fears, blockages, and barriers that impede spiritual and personal progress.

At the entrance to the Underworld stands the yew, considered the tree of death in all European countries for several reasons. The yew berry is deadly poisonous and was used to poison weapons. Yew wood is believed to make the best bows and dagger handles, and many ancient cemeteries are full of yew trees. The yew was one of the five magical trees of Ireland described as "the renown of Banbha" (a Crone or Death aspect of the Triple Goddess). The yew is very much associated with death and the Underworld aspects of the Crone Goddess, keeper of the spirits in her Underworld womb. Every ancient Irish king wore a yew brooch in the shape of a wheel to remind him of the turning of the life's wheel and the inevitability of death.

The yew, however, is also a tree of regeneration arising from death. As the central trunk becomes old and the insides decay, a new tree grows within the spongy dying mass of the old. In Brittany, it is said that a churchyard yew will send a root to the mouth of each corpse. This root is a symbol of the spirit reborn in much the same way as the tree is reborn.

The border of the card depicts two dragons. For the Megalithic people, the dragon represented the energy of the earth, stretching across the country in dragon or ley lines and occasionally centered in spirals and whorls marked with circles and standing stones that tapped into their power. Such concentrations of earth energy were often given place names relating to the dragon or worm, such as Dragon Hill, and Christianized by being dedicated to dragon slaying saints, such as St. George or St. Michael. In myth, dragons often guard a treasure in a deep cave. The treasures they guard are the energy of the earth and the secrets of the Goddess—her mysteries of life and death. They also guard the storehouse of the unconscious mind.

Divinatory Meanings

The Underworld is the hidden realm within, where your self-created inner demons dwell—your deepest fears, hatreds, prejudices, and feelings of self-disgust. Here lives the secret dark half of yourself, the shadow side, which lies buried and suppressed in the darkest recesses of the subconscious mind, yet holds you in bondage, affecting every thought process and action and preventing you from moving forward free and unchained.

Deep down, everyone shares the same fears—fear of death, fear of being hurt, fear of suffering, fear of loneliness—these are survival instincts and part of the human makeup. However, conditioning and life experience often twist these natural instincts and bind them with inappropriate associations.

When the Underworld card appears in your spread, you are being asked to look at your subconscious motivations. You are being held prisoner by your inner fears or by a suppressed experience that you refuse to face and deal with. This inappropriate response is weakening you and putting you in danger of becoming an emotional cripple. You may feel a rage that is inappropriately expressed, or your violence—emotional or physical—may be directed at yourself. You may be punishing yourself for things that were not your fault.

Reverse Meanings

The Underworld reversed is a card of abuse. You may have been abused or are abusing your power over others to get your own way, irrespective of their feelings. Your ambition may be so dominating that you are prepared to use unscrupulous methods to achieve your ends and to trample over anyone who gets in your way. You may be obsessed with money and possessions to the extent that nothing else seems important; even other people are counted as possessions.

The Journey of the Fool

The crisis of death has brought the fool to the gates of the Under-world, where he must journey to the center of the life maze. But first he must pass the Guardian of the Threshold.

It is the Dark Self that is described as the Guardian of the Threshold in occult terms, who bars the way to further progress, and ultimately initiation, until he is dealt with. The Guardian can adopt terrifying and monstrous forms, which are personifications of deeply buried fears. Worldwide, shamans and witches describe the initiatory process as a series of journeys into the Underworld, where frightening monsters must be fought and defeated. It is a frightening thing to be brought face to face with your most severely repressed fears—something that everyone would prefer not to do, would prefer not to know about. However, it is this Dark Self that opens the gateway to initiation, and the guardian is not defeated by repression or by being fought, but by being recognized and assimilated as part of the whole Self. It is this whole Self that is the treasure the dragon guards.

The Tower

The card depicts a high tower struck by lightning. The borders of the card show rowan berries and a snake.

The Symbolism

The actual tower depicted in this card is one at Glendalough in County Wicklow, Ireland. It is the site of a monastic settlement, founded by St. Caoimhghin. The saint is said to have been born without any pain to his mother and was nourished by a mysterious white cow. An angel told him to go to Gleann Da Loch, the valley of the two lakes, and found a monastery. He banished a great monster from the larger lake, and at the smaller lake, men and beasts could be healed as the monster took on their illnesses.

Like many British and Irish saints, St. Caoimhghin has obviously taken on many aspects of earlier Celtic deities. In mythology, gods and goddesses are often nurtured by otherworldly cattle, and water is associated with the healing power of the Goddess.

In this card, the tower depicts a man-made structure symbolic of the concepts one builds up around oneself, the attitudes, ambitions, and lifestyle. The tower is struck by lightning, which can represent an outside agency or divine intervention.

The ancients saw the lightning as the divine strike of the sky god, and it was called the sky-serpent or lightning-snake. The thunderstorm was believed to be the mating of the Sky Father and the Earth Mother bringing the fertilizing rain. The lightning strike itself was a phallic thrust of fertilizing power.

Many so-called "serpent plants," plants (including several mushrooms) given the title of "serpent" or "snake" for their ability to alter consciousness, have been used shamanically to bring about trance states and engender Otherworld journeys. The Druids used snake stones, said to be formed by adders breathing on hazel wands, for healing and divination.

The snake is seen as a link with the Underworld from its habit of living in the earth, privy to the secrets of the Goddess and slain and resurrected gods. Snakes were often found in graveyards and were thought to be communicating with the dead or to be the dead, themselves. The serpent or dragon is seen as guarding a wealth of Underworld treasure under a lake, in a cave, or an island in the far west of the ocean. The treasure is the hidden unconscious self and the Goddess' secrets of life, death, and rebirth.

In lore, the snake appearing as a trial refers to an initiation test of the candidate's abilities to defeat his own fears and restrictions. The monster snake appears as a trial that must be overcome by heroes such as Cuchulain, Fionn, and Conall Cernach. The snake also represents the life, symbolic death, and rebirth into new consciousness of the initiate.

Symbolically, the monster snake demonstrates that all aspects of life stand equally, even those things viewed as unpleasant and poisonous. If they are accepted as part of the whole, the Dance of Life, they can be assimilated and transmuted to positive benefits.

The bottom left-hand corner of the card is decorated with rowan berries. Rowan is associated with witchcraft, protection, divination, and the dead. The berries are marked with the pentagram and constitute part of the red food of the dead at Samhain, when the Mighty Dead are sought for their guidance. Magical berries appear in legend with the ability to lengthen life. In the legend of Froath, rowan berries were guarded by a dragon and were said to give sustenance equal to nine ordinary meals. It was sacred to the druids and is called "the druid's tree." The Welsh brewed a visionary drink from the rowan, and the druids spread bulls' hides over rowan wattles to travel to other realms to gain knowledge.

Divinatory Meanings

The tower in this card represents all of the things you have built up around yourself, the exterior face you present to the world.

When this card appears in your spread, it indicates that an unexpected shock or disaster will change your life completely. Some action you have taken in the past is now beginning to have unfortunate consequences that you never imagined. The tower that you have so carefully created will be destroyed no matter what you do—your plans and ambitions will be shattered.

The tower cracks and falls because it was a flawed structure built with the poor materials of misguided ambition, false values, and pride. While the consequences of this card are painful and unwanted at the time, they force you to face up to the fact that you have been deceiving yourself and living your life on a false premise. Now, you must sort through the wreckage and truthfully examine your motives. This can be a card of liberation, depending on how you respond to the situation. You have the opportunity to begin again and base your future structure on honesty, truth, and sound principles. If you try to erect the same tower again from the old rubble, it will collapse again.

Reverse Meanings

The Tower card reversed indicates a drastic, unexpected change in circumstances that cannot be altered or countered. Depending on the surrounding cards, it can indicate bankruptcy or a loss of employment. Occasionally, it can mean imprisonment, but usually it means being restricted by circumstances.

The Journey of the Fool

The Fool has undergone his symbolic death and is engaged in his journey through the Underworld, where he seeks the center of the labyrinth. At the gates of the Underworld, he had to encounter the Guardian of the Threshold, his subconscious shadow-self, which he had to learn to embrace and assimilate before he could pass. Because of this, his carefully constructed tower of self-image and protective delusion collapses and falls, leaving him naked and defenseless, for the first time conscious of his whole, true Self.

The collapse of the tower is echoed in descriptions of shamanic initiation, where the candidate experiences in a vision a symbolic dismemberment whereby his body is stripped down to its bones.

Initiation

The card shows the initiatory maze with the cauldron of rebirth and inspiration at its center. A woodpecker rises from the smoke. The border bears the hazel nuts of wisdom and chervil herb.

The Symbolism

Initiation is a ritual death, renewal, and rebirth. It is not a single event, nor is it conferred by a ceremony—it is a continuous journey of expanding consciousness. The journey is symbolized by the double spiral, which first curves inward, the declining death spiral to the center—the point of initiation and renewal. It then moves outward, the unfolding spiral of new life. During the process of initiation, the candidate undergoes the death of his old self and travels to the Underworld following in the footsteps of the God at Herfest. He leaves behind his previous world view, what he was before he "died," as he re-enters the womb of the Mother. There he is tested and refined to prove his worthiness to enter the cauldron of renewal and come to rebirth, as the God does at Yule, sharing a new world view. Because of his rebirth, he is called the twice-born. Each individual repeats this process and brings it alive in his or her own body, the human journey as a mirror of the Divine Quest and the cycle of the year. Before the mysteries, the candidate stands alone.

Often, initiation is marked by a ceremony that is a confirmation of what has happened or of what is happening within. In ancient times, this might involve the candidate groping in darkness through a labyrinth or maze, following the inward curving widdershins spiral of death toward the center of the maze where all things meet (like the center of the magician's circle), the point of illumination and rebirth. From then on, he would follow the unfolding outward deosil spiral of his new life.

In Britain, the long barrow tombs of the Megalithic people became vessels of initiation for living candidates. When a sacred king died, he was buried in a long barrow in the fetal position, the barrow being both the tomb in which his dead body was laid and the womb of the earth Goddess, where he awaited his rebirth. A living initiatory candidate would enter the barrow tomb, enacting a symbolic death, and lie in the dark womb of the Goddess, waiting for his vision of illumination, an experience of the unity of the cosmos, the web in its totality. Afterward, he would crawl out of the tunnel at the front of the barrow, which represented the birth canal, his symbolic rebirth from the Mother. The Otherworld traveler emerged into a new state of understanding: certain events, experiences, and visions having conferred knowledge that permanently altered his outlook on the everyday world, his entire being having been changed, re-polarized.

In many cultures, the candidate would be given a special potion or drink containing sacred herbs, enabling him to experience visions and many levels of consciousness, as we saw in the card of the Shaman. The cauldron represented in this card, however, is far more profound. It is the womb of the Goddess, which is the source of all life and reabsorbs all souls in death before bringing them to rebirth.

The card shows a woodpecker rising from the cauldron. The bird is thought to be a herald of rebirth as it climbs trees in a sunwise spiral. In stories, the woodpecker knows where treasure is hidden and the location of the mysterious herb springwort, which could open doors and locks—not physical doors and locks, but spiritual ones opening the way to the true Self. The herb must be earned, and the woodpecker pecks out the eyes of anyone who tries to steal it.

Chervil is one of the sacred herbs of initiation; it bears five seeds, the sacred Goddess number, and is dedicated to the Goddess Ceridwen and the secret of her cauldron, which can both be seen as her earth-womb of regeneration and as the healing herbs it brings forth, which forever change the consciousness of the initiate. It reminds us of the immortality of the soul through the cycle of life, death, and rebirth, and is used to attune to the Higher Self.

Nuts are a Celtic symbol of concentrated wisdom, the sweetness of knowledge contained, compact in a hard shell, hence the expression "the matter in a nutshell." The hazel was associated with sacred springs and wells believed to be entrances to the Otherworld.

Divinatory Meanings

In many cultures, rites of passage mark the transition from one period of life to another, for example, a girl's first menstruation and her transition to womanhood, or marriage, the transition from the single life to the married one, and so on. This is one kind of initiation, the passage from one state to a new one.

When the Initiation card appears in your spread, it may mark such a transition, the nature of which can be divined from surrounding cards. The woodpecker signifies that one cycle has ended and another is about to begin. The success of any enterprise depends on cooperation with and consideration for others. Existing relationships can reach new levels of happiness and fulfillment by taking time to understand and accept the feelings of your partner.

A spiritual initiation also marks the passage from one state to another, a state of new consciousness. When the Initiation card appears in your spread, it marks the dawning of spiritual awareness and joy. This is a card of balance and harmony derived from working with sympathetic people in a relationship of equal give and take.

Reverse Meanings

When the Initiation card appears reversed in your spread, it indicates a lack of balance. You are trying to fill up your life with activities to disguise the fact that something fundamental is missing. Any knowledge you gain is only superficial, because you are a butterfly and cannot settle on one thing long enough to make any real progress with it. Take heed of the lessons of the woodpecker.

Woodpecker is a forest spirit, wise in the ways of the wildwood. It knows the ways of all the animals and plants and their habits at all times of the year. Woodpecker is a guide to the natural world. He is often the familiar of the herbalist, leading the way to the plants that heal both the body and the spirit. Woodpecker is particularly helpful in discerning the emotional causes of illness—such as the anger that is often the seed of arthritis, the negativity that is the root of cancer, and so on—and discovering methods of dealing with these. The spirit and the body are connected, and dis-ease in one will manifest in the other. Woodpecker makes a good visualization tool for releasing pain and negativity.

The Journey of the Fool

In this card, the fool has reached the center of the labyrinth, where the cauldron of regeneration and rebirth lies. Here he must allow himself to be reabsorbed into the womb of the Goddess by dissolving himself in the cauldron, allowing the elements of his being to return to the source and become one with Goddess once more—free, formless, and unlimited. The Druid Gwion described himself as having been in the womb of Ceridwen nine months before being reborn as Taliesin, or Radiant Brow, meaning "an enlightened one." The fool will be renewed by the Goddess, reformed and reborn, and must now begin the outward journey of the initiation spiral, a difficult journey in which he must absorb and apply the lessons he has learned.

The Star

This card shows a bright, glimmering star in the night sky over a stone circle in which a fire burns. The borders of the card are decorated with rowan and periwinkle.

The Symbolism

For the ancients, the sky and the stars were a manifestation of the divine powers at work. They marked the passage of time and foretold the destinies of humankind. This was the celestial realm, the home of the sky gods—heaven. According to the ancient art of astrology, the fate of humanity is determined and influenced by the movements of the stars as the sun passes through each sign of the zodiac during the year. It is as if the universe is the last visible layer of creation beyond which the mind cannot penetrate or imagine.

The ancients used stone circles, properly aligned, to predict the equinoxes and solstices, solar and lunar eclipses, and so on. These circles were designed to draw power from the heavens to earth.

In the circle, the pole star remains fixed above its northern quarter and the other stars seem to revolve around it as a fixed axis, rising and setting with the seasons. It was thought to be the hub of the wheel of the heavens as it did not itself rise or set below the horizon, even at the midsummer solstice.

It is also the home of the goddess Arianrhod, "Silver Wheel," a goddess of birth, initiation, and reincarnation. She is a weaver goddess, and hers is the spiral thread of life that leads to the labyrinth of the stars and outward again. Caer Arianrhod, the circumpolar stars, was thought to be the Spiral Castle of death and rebirth to which the soul journeys at death to rest between incarnations and from which it emerges in rebirth. It is also where the spirit of the initiate journeys in order to learn. Taliesin stated that he had been three times in the Spiral Castle, or in other words had undergone a threefold initiation.

Two plants are depicted in the border of the card: rowan and periwinkle. The rowan is associated with the protection of souls in the Underworld, while the periwinkle is a plant sacred to the Goddess teaching of our connection with the web of life and death. It is used in funeral rites to hasten the progress of the soul to the Otherworld.

Divinatory Meanings

The Star is a pale light in the darkness—hope. It is a fundamental facet of human nature that even when problems seem overwhelming we can still feel hope; perhaps it is part of our survival instinct. Those with hope will always fare better than those without it, whether they are ill or subject to otherwise insufferable circumstances. Hope can sometimes seem to work miracles.

This card is the herald of a new beginning instigated by an experience that will give you new hope in the future, an inspiration that will give you the courage and strength to go on. Your horizons will broaden and you will feel a renewed mental and physical vigor. It may be that you will receive help from unexpected quarters, or the support of good friends will renew your faith in human nature. Though any long-term plans will not be clear at this point, you can arise like the fabled phoenix from the ashes of your unhappy past as long as you have hope and faith in the future.

Spiritually, you will be fortified by your love of humanity, by keeping your faith strong, and by trusting in your spiritual insight. The Star card indicates that you will experience moments of illumination and great clarity of vision.

Reverse Meanings

When the Star card appears reversed in your spread, it is telling you that you are being stubborn, that you have settled into a rigid and inflexible way of thinking that makes you unwilling or incapable of adapting to changing circumstances. A lot of useful opportunities are passing you by because you do not trust other people and because you doubt your own abilities. You need to change your attitudes. Try starting slowly by doing a few things you wouldn't normally do, whether it is taking up a sport or a new hobby, or getting involved in a charity. Learn to relax—and most of all, learn to laugh and play.

The Journey of the Fool

The Fool has journeyed to the center of the labyrinth, the tower of his false self-image destroyed along the way. After his immersion in the cauldron of inspiration, he now sees a guiding light that will lead him out of the darkness of the Underworld into the full light of his spiritual realization. The unfolding spiral of his initiation has begun.

The star is often seen as an archetype of the developing true Self; the process of the integration of the ego and the soul at a deeper level of consciousness; the realization of the wholeness and oneness of the mind, body, and spirit—a personal microcosm of the totality of the cosmos.

The Moon

The card shows the Imbolc full moon over the West Kennet Long Barrow. Bats fly in the night sky and a moth perches in the corner. In the foreground are the early snowdrops of spring.

The Symbolism

The moon was the first method used to calculate time, with its waxing and waning periods. The root word for *moon* still gives us our words *month*, *measurement*, and *menstruation*. The moon was a powerful image for the Stone Age people and embodied a central mystery, changeless but ever-changing. The phases of the moon could be seen as reflected in the life of women and the Great Goddess herself, the waxing moon as maiden, full moon as pregnant mother, the waning moon as an old woman.

The moon has four phases—three visible (waxing, full, and waning), and then three days in darkness. It could be imagined that the dark phase was the invisible dimension where life gestated and renewal occurred. This was identified with life on earth; all things emerged from the darkness of the womb and grew to fullness before aging and dying. Thus, an invisible order governed the phases of the moon and the cycle of the year, the seasons, and the life of man.

Seeds were sown in the earth womb of the Goddess, who brought them to life and nurtured them into growth. Her bounty then nurtured the population as food. She blessed women and animals with young. The seed and the dead were laid back in her fruitful womb at death, from whence she brought them to rebirth.

In this card, the moon shines full above the West Kennet Long Barrow, a chambered Neolithic tomb situated in Wiltshire, England, near Silbury Hill and the Avebury stone circle. Just as the seed enters the dark earth and emerges from it in the spring, in the darkness of the tomb, the soul moves toward rebirth. Death and darkness are not to be feared, but are an essential part of the cycle; all are aspects of the nurturing Goddess. Light and darkness, life and death, are not opposites but follow each other in season—a part of the whole.

A bat hovers above the tomb. Because of its nocturnal habits, the bat is associated with the night and the powers of darkness. In Scotland, it was thought that if a bat flew swiftly upward, then downward, the witching hour was at hand.

The bat is a symbol of initiation. The bat hangs in dark caves upside down, acting as a symbol of the transformation of the self into a new being with a new viewpoint; this is, of course, also the position that babies assume when they leave the womb.

The bat is often the familiar of the witch. According to the old teachings, a bat familiar may show you how to move through the twilight as a doorway to other realms, how to fly your dreams. Bat teaches you how to refine your mind to experience new levels of consciousness, how to shift perspective and see things in a different way. Perhaps one of the most important lessons of the bat is how to sift illusion from reality, to know when a true lesson has been taught rather than when you are fooling yourself with wishful thinking.

A moth perches on the border of the card. In Europe, the moth is a symbol of the soul and attraction to the light. Many believe that white moths are the souls of the dead and that it is unlucky to kill one.

The snowdrop is the first flower of spring, flowering around Imbolc (Candelmas) and associated in modern Druidic lore with that festival. As such it symbolizes purity and the cleansing of the earth's face after winter. It represents the coming of light and growth during the time of darkness.

Divinatory Meanings

The Moon card speaks of the mystery of regeneration—the monthly renewal of the moon, the yearly renewal of the earth, the cyclical renewal of the spirit, and the reincarnation of the soul. All things move from the darkness into the light and pass back into the darkness once more.

Our ancient ancestors believed that it was during the dark time of the moon that its regeneration took place, and during the darkness of winter that the regeneration of the earth took place as it prepared itself to emerge in the spring; to be laid in the darkness of the tomb was to be laid in the womb of the Goddess, where the soul readied itself for rebirth.

When the Moon card appears in your spread, it indicates that this is a period of change and fluctuation; nothing remains stable or certain for long. The Moon calls on you to accept change and the cycles of life. It is time for something buried deep in your subconscious to be brought out into the light. It may be that you need to let go of something—a bad habit, a negative thought pattern, a destructive relationship, or an old hurt that is holding you back and stopping you from developing as you need to. You must change your attitudes; you are causing yourself pain. You cannot live in the past, but must continue to grow and face the future. What does not change stagnates.

The Moon is a fortuitous card for writers and artists. It indicates bringing ideas from the subconscious to manifest as works of fiction, poetry, paintings, and sculpture. Artists call on their most painful experiences to inform their work, and writing down or drawing your problems may help to expiate them.

Spiritually, this card calls on you to pay attention to what your dreams are trying to tell you. This is also an excellent time to develop your psychic skills. You will be more intuitive than usual and should trust your instincts.

Reverse Meanings

When the Moon card appears reversed in your spread, it indicates that you have been deceiving yourself. You are trying to hide from reality in the world of fantasy and daydreams. Perhaps you have also been lying to other people and find it hard to stop. The moon is warning you that this situation is self-destructive and you must put it right before matters are taken out of your hands.

The Journey of the Fool

The fool is engaged in the outward spiral of his initiatory process and has been following the pale light of the star as his guide through the labyrinth. Now he encounters the primordial power of the moon, which calls moisture from the earth as refreshing dew, which governs the tides of the oceans—which endlessly generate life and reabsorb it in death—and the cycles of women's wombs, readied each month to accept the fertilization of life.

On a magical level, the moon influences and represents the collective sea of the unconscious that contains and feeds all the experiences of humankind, communicated only by symbol and legend. The fool realizes that though his journey has been an individual one, it is reflected in the journey of all souls. His own experience has contributed to the evolution of humanity as a tiny part of the whole. He has been re-enacting the eternal myth.

The Sun

The card shows the bright face of the Sun God at the height of his powers at the midsummer solstice. His warming rays ripen a summer meadow. Lizards bask in the heat and bees pollinate the flowers of St. John's wort.

The Symbolism

The sun represents both the daylight world and the inner light. While the moon rules the night and the unconscious, the sun rules the day and the conscious.

The sun passes through the procession of the zodiac during the year and its progress is marked at the stations of the equinoxes and solstices. Its zenith is midsummer, its nadir midwinter. At midsummer the sun is seen as the power of God resplendent; at Yule, it is the dying God who will be reborn the next day as a babe of Ceridwen.

In the old British Craft, the drawing down of the sun is as important as the drawing down of the moon. While the moon's image is captured in a boat of glass, the sun is concentrated on a lens and projected onto tinder, causing a flame to be lit from the divine sun. This is called wildfire, elf-fire, or need fire, and this direct method is especially sacred for lighting festival and sacred fires—the balefires or needfires. Fire is a protection against evil and a means of purification. Fire produced by the friction of two pieces of special wood has the same value, or fires caused by lightning. It has a celestial, and therefore a magically potent, origin.

Basking in the light of the sun are two lizards. The lizard's names in Welsh, *Lleufer*, and Gaelic, *Bog-luachair*, associate it with light. The lizard is sun-loving, it hibernates and re-emerges in the spring. In Europe, it was thought to go blind during this period and emerge still blind in the spring, until it climbs on an east-facing wall and looks east to the sunrise, and thus has its sight restored. All lizards have a residual third eye, and in some species this eye can detect changes in light conditions. Because of this, lizards are associated with wisdom and divination, with Otherworldly methods of discovering secrets.

Bees are also considered wise creatures with special knowledge of the future. They are meant to know all the old lore and are associated with divine inspiration. A Scottish saying goes "Ask the wild bee for what the Druids knew," and the Celts believed they held secret wisdom derived from the Underworld.

In this card, a bee is shown pollinating one of the most sacred herbs of midsummer, the St. John's wort. It is a plant of the sun and magically encompasses the sun's energy; it is especially empowered at the summer solstice when it is cut with a bronze knife at midday and used for purification and protection.

Divinatory Meanings

The rising of the sun dispels the darkness and its light reveals the pattern of the landscape, warming and nurturing the life it contains. Though life is gestated in the darkness, it strives toward the light, just as the human consciousness strives toward illumination.

From now on, you will be able to see things clearly and plan with confidence. You feel optimistic and experience a renewed energy. It may be that you will enjoy good health or recover from an illness. Use your intelligence and you can achieve any ambition you set your mind to, from inventing something new to achieving academic acclaim. At this propitious time, all your efforts will be rewarded by financial gain or the recognition of your peers.

On a spiritual level, this card indicates a great leap forward. Your consciousness will be illuminated by a new and deeper understanding. Things that have seemed shadowy, indistinct, or irrelevant suddenly become clear and fall into place. Follow the example of the lizard. Lizard can see into the Otherworld and teaches the art of attaining the ability to enter into a trance state, of being able to shift the consciousness just enough to see as the seer does. Lizard is master of all the arts of divination.

Reverse Meanings

The Sun card reversed is advising you that your intelligence is not being usefully directed. It may be that you are fantasizing about success rather than doing anything to achieve it, or muddled thinking has led to a serious misjudgment. Lack of communication leads to problems with legal contracts, marriages, and partnerships.

You are feeling very sensitive, you are rushing around and not achieving anything. Slow down and listen to the lesson of the lizard. You need to look inward, spend some time in meditation and take note of what is revealed to you, then apply it to your life. A germinating shoot that is brought too soon into the heat of the sun will shrivel and die. Your ideas will have a better chance of working if you allow them time to gestate and grow instead of thrusting them prematurely into the glaring light of public gaze.

This reversed card sometimes indicates learning difficulties, either your own or your children's, owing not to a lack of intelligence but rather to inappropriate teaching methods.

The Journey of the Fool

The Fool has completed his terrifying and perilous journey through the darkness of the Underworld, sustained only by the strength and determination of his spirit. Like all things, his True Self gestated and grew in the dark and strove toward the light. Now the bright light of the sun dispels the shadows and the last of his fears and he is ready to emerge into the daylight world with his new knowledge and his new consciousness.

Rebirth

The card shows the sun, reborn as a babe of Ceridwen after the winter solstice, rising through a dolmen arch that is inscribed with spiral patterns and decorated with holly and ivy.

The Symbolism

This card illustrates the rebirth of the sun after the winter solstice which is sometimes called Yule—derived from *yul*, meaning *wheel*. Solstice means "sun stands still," and in the northern hemisphere, the winter solstice occurs when we are tilted at the farthest point from the sun. It is the shortest day, with only about six hours of daylight, and the longest night of the year. After the winter solstice, the days lengthen and the sun grows stronger, until its zenith at the midsummer solstice, the longest day and shortest night.

To many the sun was, or represented, a god. The diminishing of his warmth and light was seen as his sickness and decline toward death. It was important to banish the darkness before the sun disappeared forever. For the ancients, the rebirth of the sun was by no means certain. Humans believed that they took part in the cycle of the wheel and their actions affected it; their efforts were needed to turn it and ensure the regeneration of the god. Unless prayers were said, ceremonies performed, and sacrifices made, there would be no return of the sun, no summer, no harvest.

Winter was a dangerous time, not only because of the threat of death by cold or starvation, but because during the dark days between Samhain and Yule the gates to the Underworld stood open and the dead walked the land. It was a time for ghosts, werewolves, evil spirits, and the Wild Hunt. Charms and spells were needed to protect people, animals, and property. Fire was needed to push back the darkness. Fire is younger brother to the sun, and fires were lit as a sympathetic magic to encourage the sun to strengthen and begin the long climb back to midsummer. Red was worn to give strength to the sun, and people would dance around the fire, clad in deerskins and antlers, goat hides, horse head skulls, and masks. To keep the vegetation spirit alive, houses were decorated with evergreens—holly, ivy, and mistletoe. Evergreens had great magical power as they could withstand the winter death.

The Celts regarded the sun that rose on the day before the solstice as a shadow sun, the real sun having been imprisoned by the King of the Underworld. In a year of thirteen solar months of twenty-eight days apiece, there is a day left over, a crack between the worlds and a time of chaos, a nameless day. The Celts called this season Alban Arthur, Arthur's season, when the sun god fought the powers of darkness until the new sun was born from between the horns of the moon as a babe of Ceridwen.

In the European traditions, gods of the sun and light are nearly all said to have been born from a cave at the midwinter solstice. Many burial chambers, such as the one at Newgrange in Ireland, are oriented to the rising of the winter solstice sun. The sun illuminates the inner chamber and appears to re-emerge from it, as though being born from the cave womb of the Goddess. Spirals and mazes carved at Newgrange, where the sun god Lugh is reputed to be buried, depict the path of the sun and the human spirit, spiralling down to death and out again to its rebirth, a theme echoed in the seasonal ivy, a symbol of life and rebirth as it grows spirally and remains green throughout the winter.

The Goddess giving birth to the new sun is represented by the traditional carvings of the Sheila-na-gig, who cheekily managed to keep appearing in Christian churches.

Divinatory Meanings

This is the card of rebirth, though in most tarot packs it is called "Judgement" and portrays the dead rising from their graves on the Day of Judgement, when according to Christian thought, souls will receive their final reward or punishment according to a person's conduct in life. However, in Pagan philosophy the eternal spirit evolves through several lifetimes, undergoing many cycles of birth, life, and death, and journeying toward rebirth once again, hopefully learning and growing with each incarnation. In view of this, the Rebirth card has a much more profound meaning. It is the promise of the Eternal Return, just as the rebirth of the sun at Yule promises the return of spring, so the soul is promised new life, that the wheel of death and rebirth shall level all things in the end.

On a divinatory level, this card reflects the Craft law that all actions, whether good or evil, are repaid in kind and carry the seeds of their own justice. At this point in time, your past actions are shaping your present and you will be rewarded or punished accordingly. When this card appears upright, it indicates that some experience will impel you to review your past in an attempt to discern the pattern of your life and the choices you made to bring you to your present point. With this information, you will have a new viewpoint with which to approach the future. This is a card of change and renewal. You will move forward with new energy and resolution; this card always represents a definite step. Depending on surrounding cards, the Rebirth card can herald the recovery of your health and vitality.

On a spiritual level, this card heralds a profound change in your consciousness. Your insight reveals that the person you are now is the result of past actions and choices. Previously unrecognized patterns are made clear and are seen as part of the whole.

Reverse Meanings

The Rebirth card reversed indicates that the time has come when you will have to answer for your past decisions. You have not been true to yourself—though you are an expert at self-deception, you are consumed with guilt and fear.

You will have to take the consequences of your actions—they cannot be avoided—but this card advises you to look honestly at what has brought you to this point. Stop trying to fool yourself and avoid the issue. If you can truthfully discern your motivations, you can move forward into the future with a new insight.

This card can sometimes indicate illness and the fear of death. This is a natural apprehension, but one that can grow to overwhelming and debilitating proportions, sometimes with little or no foundation. Fear is the great destroyer of the mind, body, and spirit, while hope nurtures and renews. However, fear cannot be sustained indefinitely and eventually ceases to become fear. It either transforms into desolation and despair worse than a living death, or into a spur to action, the resolution to live until you die, as we all must, whatever happens.

The Journey of the Fool

With this card, the Fool has completed the outward spiral of his initiation. All his lessons have been absorbed. In many ways, this was the hardest part of his journey; his world view was totally altered and the struggle to center himself in the new consciousness was very difficult. Like many new initiates, he has experienced confusion, alienation, and depression while the integration took place and his journey from the cauldron has taken several years. Now the unfolding of the initiation into waking consciousness and everyday life has come to fruition and he acts from a new perspective.

The World Tree

The card shows the World Tree, a giant oak that links the Three Realms of Being. The sacred mistletoe hangs from its branches. The landscape behind the tree shows the midsummer sunrise on one side and the winter full moon on the other. An eagle circles the skies and a snake slithers through the roots of the tree.

The Symbolism

In magical terms, the Three Realms are connected by the *axis mundi* or World Tree. The tree has its roots in the Underworld, its trunk in Middle Earth, and its branches in the heavens. The concept of the cosmos as a tree is widespread in Pagan mythology. The best known example is the Scandinavian Yggdrasil, a giant evergreen ash tree. For the Celts, the World Tree was an apple or oak.

Middle Earth is the realm in which we live—the earth, the physical plane, the realm of ordinary consciousness. The Craft teaches that we should not try to escape this realm, that it is not base and a place of evil, but that it is good and beautiful. We should learn to interact fully with it, care for it, and love it, for the Divine is manifest within it. We are part of it. Through the study of the earth, of nature and its cycles, we learn of the great cosmic patterns. Through the study and practice of life and magic, we interact with them.

From the earth we begin, and in touch with the earth we can contact other realities. However, we must always be in touch with the earth and our physical existence.

In popular modern thought, the Underworld is associated with the Christian concept of hell—a place of evil, darkness, and punishment. However, for the ancients and for Pagans it does not have these connotations. The Underworld is as much a realm of the Goddess as the earth and heaven. The Underworld can be seen as the womb of the Dark Mother, the primal matter from which all life issues.

It is to this dark realm that the seeker travels in search of answers to fundamental questions at the root of being. The Underworld is viewed as the source of ancestral or primal knowledge and the place where this may be accessed. In human terms, it corresponds to the subconscious or unconscious level of the mind. Through the Underworld is the access to the Self.

The celestial realm is the home of the sky gods. It represents the aspirations of the spirit and the highest levels of consciousness to which the initiate travels after his immersion in the cauldron of rebirth. It has different lessons to teach from those accessible in the Underworld or Middle Earth.

The World Tree of the Druids was the oak. Its roots extend as far underground as the branches do above. As such, it is a symbol of the law "as above, so below." The oak is an *axis mundi* tree, representing the connection between the three realms and is a doorway to the Otherworld.

In the Wheel of the Year, the oak plays a part at both midsummer, when it flowers, and midwinter when the mistletoe is cut from its branches.

There is mistletoe growing on the oak in this picture, which in reality is a rare and special event. Mistletoe was a sacred herb of the druids and known as *druad-lus,* meaning "the druid's plant." Around the winter solstice, six days after the new moon, a druid on one leg, with one arm raised and with one eye closed (i.e., not wholly standing in this world, and one eye looking into the inner world) would cut the mistletoe, at one stroke, with a golden sickle. The sickle represented the sun's energy and the moon's substance. The mistletoe was seen as the semen of the oak, its vitality, and this was used to strengthen the sun in its weakened state. To the druids, it symbolized life through death.

In the sky above the oak an eagle flies. Its power and strength associate it with authority and royalty; Scottish chieftains wore three eagle feathers in their bonnets, as do fairy princes in legend. In Britain, the eagle is known as the King of the Birds. It is a solar symbol, representing both temporal and spiritual power. The eagle was thought to renew itself by flying to the sun and scorching its feathers before plunging into the sea to emerge as a young bird, thus making it an emblem of the resurrection of the spirit, renewal, and the power of life over death.

Eagle is King of the Air and perches in the topmost branches of the World Tree, surveying all that passes beneath. Eagle is the only bird that dwells in the upper realm of the gods. For the Celts, the salmon and the eagle were the oldest animals on earth, repositories of all history, new and ancient knowledge, and seers of all that occurred in any of the realms. Eagle soars upward into the heavens, wheeling on currents of air, the element of inspiration. It teaches of the triumph of the eternal spirit, it is the guide to the highest levels of consciousness and teaches the spirit to soar.

In myth, the eagle is seen to be in conflict with the serpent of the lower realms, the Underworld, representing the dynamic equilibrium between light and darkness, summer and winter, life and death.

Mother Earth sustains us, and the snake usually lives within the earth, within the body of the Mother, and is aware of all her secrets, including those of life, death, and rebirth.

The snake is identified with the transformative energy of the Wheel of the Year. Because it sheds its skin and emerges renewed, it is seen as a symbol of life, death, and rebirth and can be associated with the entire cycle of the year from its birth at Yule, the stirrings of life in the earth belly of the Goddess and the power of her purifying wells and springs at Imbolc. At Ostara, the spring equinox, the Goddess lays the serpent's egg, or *glain* of the Druids, which represents the increasing power of the sun. In human form, she eats the egg and becomes pregnant with the next divine child, who is born at midwinter ten lunar months later. At Beltane, it represents the sacred marriage of the Lord and Lady, and at Coamhain (midsummer) it is a power animal of fire. At Lughnasa, it is the horned serpent that accompanies the God in his prime. At the autumn equinox the snake returns to the Underworld and the dark half of the year, and the Underworld cycle of the God begins, communing with the ancestors at Samhain.

Divinatory Meanings

The World Tree represents not only the whole cosmos, but is the central axis that links all three realms. This axis does not exist in any physical place, but can be created anywhere by the conscious will of the magician. By aligning himself or herself with the *axis mundi*, he or she is aligned with the center of the universe and through it has access to all the realms. When the circle is cast, the first act is to draw the axis down through its center and link the circle to all the realms, to be "between the worlds."

At the deepest levels of Pagan teaching, the practitioner or magician travels to various realms of consciousness in order to gain knowledge and personal teaching from Otherworldly beings.

On a mundane level, the card of the World Tree marks the successful completion of some venture, achieving something that you have worked hard for: the successful end of a cycle of events. You will be rewarded for all your efforts—it is time to celebrate. This card may also indicate a journey, either spiritual or physical, during which an important lesson will be learned.

On a higher level, the card of The World Tree demonstrates the Oneness and interconnection of all things, their equal importance and their myriad possibilities. This is an ideal, rather than something that we can attain on a day-to-day basis—we're only human, after all. However, it is something we can glimpse at certain special moments and sense its harmony, its reconciliation of opposites.

Reverse Meanings

You are ignoring the lessons that life is trying to teach you. You are projecting your internal conflicts onto other people and blaming them for your failures instead of trying to understand and solve your problems at the source. It is not weakness to admit that you might be wrong, that you might not know the answer to a question or feel unsure about the way forward—it takes great courage and is a sign of strength.

When the World Tree appears reversed in your spread, it is warning you that a situation is not resolved or a project finished, even though you might think it is.

The Journey of the Fool

The Fool has ended his journey, but now a new one begins . . . .

Minor Arcana

Swords, Wands, Cups, and Discs

Suit of Swords

Element: air

Season: spring
Imbolc to Beltane Eve

Color: yellow

Attributes: the mind, the intellect,
the power of thought to
shape your world

Direction: east

Festival: Ostara

Ace of Swords

The card shows a great, powerful, shining sword with a jewelled hilt. Waves of energy emanate from the blade. In the background is St. Michael's Mount in Cornwall, England.

The Symbolism

The Ace of Swords is the root of the powers of air. It is the magical weapon brought from the mystical city of Gorias, which no eye has seen but the soul knows. It appears in various guises as the sword Excalibur, the athame, and the curfane.

The suit of swords corresponds to the element of air, the season of spring, the dawn, and the direction of the east. Its station on the wheel is the spring equinox, which we call Ostara, when new life germinates and emerges with the increase of light and warmth. Magically, air rules all mental activity, from the inception of an idea to abstract knowledge, to the questioning of established theories.

Air is the inspiration of life-giving breath, the gentle breeze on the plain, the rushing wind on the mountain top, and the destructive hurricane. It is the power of sound, the vocalization of ideas, and the communication of knowledge.

In this card, the Ace of Swords is shown over St. Michael's Mount, a small island off the coast of Cornwall, which is linked to the mainland village of Marazion by a causeway. For the ancients, islands like St. Michael's Mount were often sites of initiation, since they were places between places—neither part of the mainland nor islands proper. It is the termination of the long ley or dragon line called the St. Michael's Line, which stretches halfway across Britain. This earth energy line is oriented to sunrise at Beltane and Lughnasa, when it is activated as the sun rises, and oriented to sunset at Imbolc and Samhain, when the energy is discharged. The southern aspect of this line is called the Great Dragon Line, where churches dedicated to St. Michael and St. George abound. Both saints are known as dragon slayers, overcoming the darkness, remembered with torches and bonfires. These ancient sites where our Pagan ancestors invoked the fertile dragon power of the earth were later superimposed with Christian churches dedicated to dragon-slaying deities, a statement that Paganism had been overcome in that area.

St. Michael is the patron saint of Cornwall and is associated with overcoming winter and death. He is said to have appeared on May 8 on St. Michael's Mount in 590 C.E. Nearby, the Helston Furry Dance—a serpentine dance that banishes winter and winds up a spiral of energy, coiling up the summer—is celebrated on May 8.

Divinatory Meanings

The aces of each of the suits represent powerful bursts of raw energy. The Ace of Swords indicates an awakening of mental powers, a surge of new ideas and concepts that will change your view of the world and your life forever.

However, the sword can be a ruthless weapon, it can cut away dead wood or living flesh. It can be used as a force for good or ill. The irresistible power of the Ace of Swords is bound to lead to some conflicts with those around you who are not willing to change so quickly, if indeed at all. History shows us that new ideas have often led to terrible wars and conflagrations, though it is sometimes out of adversity that the most creative ideas arise, and it is possible that out of present disagreements something better will be forged.

The Ace of Swords shows that you have great personal reserves of strength that you can call on to see you through present difficulties. You have the power to acquire knowledge and shape your world with your intellect.

Reverse Meanings

The Ace of Swords reversed indicates that someone is misusing their power in an attempt to hurt you, either with machinations directed at some cherished project that you are working on or at you personally. You may even be the victim of violence. You have obviously upset someone, and the best course of action would be to discover who and why and try to reach a peaceful compromise.

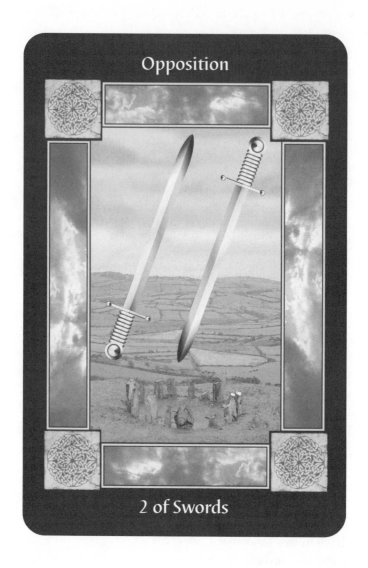

Two of Swords

The card shows two swords opposing each other. The Drombeg
Stone Circle in Ireland is in the background.

The Symbolism

The two identical bronze swords that oppose each other are equally balanced. Neither has any advantage that would enable it to overcome the other, but neither will back down and a perpetual state of warfare is maintained.

In the background is Drombeg Stone Circle in County Cork. It is aligned to the winter solstice sunset in one direction, and therefore the summer solstice in the other, representing the equal and opposed forces of winter and summer, held in eternal balance.

Divinatory Meanings

You find yourself in a stalemate situation and you are neither able to move forward nor retreat. This is not a comfortable situation, but a state of armed truce. Any quarrels you have been involved in have been superficially glossed over, but resentments and tensions still lie under the surface. At present, any efforts you make to resolve the situation will be frustrated. It is best to sit back and wait for things to blow over.

Depending on the surrounding cards, the Two of Swords may mean that you find yourself in a tricky situation, but you are unwilling to face up to sorting it out for fear of upsetting the status quo. If an adverse property card appears nearby, it could mean that you are in danger of losing your home.

Reverse Meanings

The Two of Swords reversed indicates that you have been given bad advice from a source who is either misguided or malicious. You must carefully consider the consequences of acting on any advice you have been given.

Three of Swords

The card shows three sharp swords, all slashing the air threateningly. The background is a dark and stormy sky over Snowdonia in Wales.

The Symbolism

Snowdonia is a mountainous region closely associated with King Arthur. The reign of King Arthur began when he drew the magical sword Excalibur from the stone and established the legendary realm of Logres, a golden age of peace and the fellowship of the round table, where all knights were equal.

As is often the case, all this was destroyed by the jealousy and malevolence of one man, Arthur's bastard son Mordred, who fomented mistrust and dissatisfaction in the court to break up the fellowship. Many knights and soldiers threw in their lot with Mordred as an easier option to the high principles of Arthur's rule.

As the forces drew together for the last battle, Arthur recalled that Merlin had foretold that the holy realm of Logres should pass away and the land return to darkness. As he mused, the spirit of Gawain appeared to him and prophesied that if he fought on the morrow, the kingdom and his life should be lost. Hoping to avert this, Arthur sent his faithful friend Bedivere to make a truce with Mordred.

The two armies gathered to treat, but Arthur warned his troops—"If you see a sword drawn, charge and slay the traitor Mordred, for I do not trust him"—and Mordred spoke likewise to his own men.

Arthur and Mordred met and reached an agreement, and a peace treaty was duly signed. However, it chanced that an adder came out of the heather and bit one of Mordred's knights on the heel. Without thinking, the knight drew his sword and slew the snake. When the two armies saw the flash of a blade, they cried out and fell on each other. It came about that many were killed, and Arthur and Mordred dealt each other death blows. Arthur is said to have died on Snowdon and to have been buried at Bwlch y Saethau, Pass of the Arrows. Llyn Llydaw, east of Snowdon, is one of the candidates for the lake where Bedivere is said to have thrown Arthur's sword after the king's death.

Divinatory Meanings

The Three of Swords indicates that things have reached rock bottom. Your life is taken up with quarrels and upheavals. You feel great sorrow at the dissolution of cherished friendships and relationships; partnerships are breaking up, and separations and divorce are possible. You may feel that you have reached the limits of your endurance. Do not despair, this situation has arisen because things could not go on forever as they were. Things are out in the open now and can only get better from this point.

If you work magically or spiritually with other people, this card indicates the endings of such groups and partnerships.

Reverse Meanings

The Three of Swords reversed indicates that you have been the victim of some treachery. You don't understand why this has happened or what you did to deserve it, but because of it you suffer sorrow and loss. Do not give this person the opportunity to hurt you further. Sadly, there are some people and situations you are better off without.

Four of Swords

The card shows four swords with jewelled hilts, all plunged into the ground with daisies growing around them. In the background is Newgrange in Ireland.

The Symbolism

The swords shown here are decorative or ceremonial, rather than weapons of war. They indicate that conflict has ceased and the time has come to rest after struggles.

The daisies growing up around the swords were once important plants for the war weary, used to counter the shock of battle injuries. Their old name, bruisewort, indicates their efficiency in treating bruises. For the Celts, the daisy was a symbol of light and Belenos, the god of the sun. Daisies flower roughly from equinox to equinox, marking the beginning and end of the sunnier half of the year.

In the background of the card is Newgrange, a passage grave in County Meath, Ireland, constructed around 3000 B.C.E. It is decorated with spirals, chevrons, and lozenges—symbols of rebirth and the Earth Goddess. It used to be the custom to bury people with their feet facing east, the direction of the newly risen sun, so that they might rise to their new life with the sun.

Divinatory Meanings

This card indicates that you have just gone through a period of great difficulty and that it is now time to rest after your struggles and gather your energies before you move on.

You need a quiet time alone so that you can reflect on what has happened to you and come to terms with it. It will be counter-productive at the moment to rush around, trying to keep busy or fill up your life with frenzied socializing. You need to rebuild your inner reserves before you are ready to go out into the world again. Now is not the time to make any definite plans.

It can be discerned from surrounding cards whether the Four of Swords indicates a period of recuperation after an illness, or whether an important relationship has ended and your life must be rebuilt without it. Perhaps serious quarrels have taken place and it is necessary to retreat from a situation to allow healing to take place.

Spiritually, it is time to seek solitude, even to go on a retreat. You need to spend some time alone in passive meditation. Now is not the time to attempt to work with others.

Reverse Meanings

The Four of Swords reversed indicates an enforced seclusion, rather than a voluntary one. In rare cases, and depending on surrounding cards, it can mean imprisonment. More usually it means that you have been excluded from some social group that you were once a member of. You will have to accept that this phase of your life is over and start to look forward to the new opportunities that will come in the future, though not just yet.

Five of Swords

The card shows five swords. Three whole swords oppose two broken ones. In the background is Avebury Stone Circle and in the foreground a mallow plant.

The Symbolism

In this card, two broken swords face three whole ones, which they have no chance of defeating.

In the background is Avebury, a stunning, 4,000-year-old Neolithic temple in Wiltshire, England. It covers thirty acres and the stone circle encloses a medieval village. The henge is surrounded by a bank twenty-five feet high and a ditch thirty-three feet deep. Around the circumference there once existed a hundred sarsen stones, of which only thirty-one remain today; pilfering the stones for building work began in the Middle Ages. A processional avenue called the West Kennet Way leads in from the south with one hundred pairs of stones marking it. It leads to the Sanctuary, one and a half miles away, which consisted of two stone circles and six concentric timber rings. Avebury is probably the most impressive prehistoric site in Britain, but is still only one of a number of seemingly interrelated sites in the area. It is linked to Windmill Hill, the West Kennet Long Barrow, and Silbury Hill. The Avebury complex must have been a massive undertaking, constructed as it was in a time before metal tools were available. It took a great many years, and the cooperation of thousands of people, to complete.

A mallow plant is in the foreground. While the mallow is generally used as a love and fertility herb, it also has connections with death and funerals. It dies down completely during the winter, to re-emerge in the spring.

Divinatory Meanings

This card calls upon you to recognize that you have taken on something beyond your present capabilities. Possibly you have just taken on too many obligations to fulfill any of them properly. It is no good complaining about how unfair it all is; you will have to swallow your pride and acknowledge defeat. Now you must accept your limitations and make an honest assessment of exactly what is possible before you proceed.

Depending on surrounding cards, the Five of Swords can be warning you that a malicious gossip is working behind your back to turn friends against you. This person is a coward and won't say anything to your face.

Spiritually you are forced to accept that at the present time you have limitations on what you understand and what you can do. You are trying to race too far ahead. You need to assimilate what you have learned before you move on. Perhaps you are trying to impose your half-digested ideas on other people? At the moment, you do not have the learning and authority to do this. Accepting this is a step on the road to knowledge. Knowing who you are, where you are, and what you are capable of at the present time is true wisdom.

Reverse Meanings

The Five of Swords reversed indicates that the problems and failures you are encountering are caused by your vacillations because you are afraid to act. You have fallen into the habit of expecting bad things to happen, and so they do. You seem to think everything and everyone is out to get you. One of the most fundamental personal and spiritual lessons is that negativity attracts negativity. Act positively, think positively, and speak positively and you can begin to turn the situation around. Only when you take responsibility for what happens to you, when you stop blaming others for your failures, can you begin to forge the life you want. It may help you to work on unblocking the throat chakra.

Solace

6 of Swords

Six of Swords

The card shows six swords traveling over running water, with beautiful violets and primroses growing on the banks of the stream. In the sky is a butterfly.

The Symbolism

The card shows six bright swords in a sunny, peaceful scene. They seem to travel over a gentle stream toward the lush woodlands in the distance. When water appears in a tarot card it represents the emotions and the workings of the subconscious mind. The landscape depicted is an inner one, the serenity that can be achieved with the right metal attitude, represented by the swords.

Your life is shaped by your thoughts, they determine how you view your past, how you perceive your present, and how you form your aspirations for the future. Your mind is powerful enough to change the way you think, you can learn to stop approaching life in a negative fashion and substitute a positive attitude.

Divinatory Meanings

The Six of Swords indicates moving away from difficulties, either physically or mentally. It can be a card of travel, journeying to a place where you can get away from your worries. On the other hand, the card can mean that by moving away from your problems, you gain an insight into their nature—you can see how they have arisen and devise methods of coping with them. With this mental comprehension and acceptance comes relief from anxiety, you feel the metaphorical weight lifting from your shoulders. Though this is not an unadulterated card of happiness, things do become much easier for you, particularly in the area of relationships.

On a deeper level, this card may be telling you that you need to learn techniques of positive thinking, of reinforcing positive mental attitudes.

Reverse Meanings

The Six of Swords reversed is telling you that you can only get away from your problems temporarily, perhaps by taking a holiday. However, they will still be there when you get back. It seems, at the moment, that no sooner have you dealt with one difficulty than another arises. You must try to gain some understanding of how this situation has arisen and devise positive methods of coping.

On a deeper level, the Six of Swords reversed is telling you that you must use the power of your intellect to gain control over your self-destructive impulses. Look within yourself to discover the reason you are driven to sabotage your own happiness when things seem to be going too well. Is it what you think you deserve? Do you just expect failure and provoke it before anyone else can? Are you afraid of the responsibility of success? If anyone else were doing this to you, you would be justifiably angry—so why treat yourself so badly? You need to work at learning to like yourself a little.

Seven of Swords

The card shows seven swords all arranged with their points in the center of the picture. In the background is the Uffington White Horse in Oxfordshire, England.

The Symbolism

The swords are not slashing around the air in opposition, but lie peacefully together with their points touching, demonstrating that this is not the time for battles but for conferences and treaties.

In the background is the Uffington White Horse. Though there are many chalk horse carvings on the hillsides of Britain, this is the oldest, constructed around 1400 B.C.E. Horses were sacred both to the Celts and the aboriginal peoples of Britain. They are swift and strong, and their domestication enabled humankind to perform previously impossible tasks, including distant travel and the spread of civilizations.

Horses are also symbolic of travel to the Otherworld. The Celts believed that the souls of the dead traveled to the afterlife on horseback. Gods and shamans tether their horses to the World Tree, the *axis mundi*, through which journeys to the Otherworld are possible. The most famous horse in Irish myth is Aonbharr, the mount of the sea god Manannan, who made her rider invulnerable. She carried the hero Conan to the Otherworld. Thomas the Rhymer was taken to the realm of the fairy by the milk-white steed of the elf queen, and Tam Lin escaped from the fairy realm on a stolen white horse.

Some say that the Uffington Horse is really a dragon, as it looks down on the Dragon Hill, where St. George is reputed to have slain the dragon. There is a bare patch on top of the hill, where nothing will grow, said to have been caused by the poisonous dragon's blood. Though the horse is a Celtic carving, it is suggested that the site may have held importance in Neolithic times as part of a ley (dragon power) network. A Bronze Age burial mound has been excavated near the head of the horse and he looks down on the Ridgeway, an ancient path that crosses southern England from Dover to Ilchester in Somerset. Wayland's Smithy, a Neolithic burial chamber, is only about a mile from the horse and, according to legend, its magical smith made the horseshoes for the giant horse.

Divinatory Meanings

The Seven of Swords advises you that cooperation is required in dealing with the present situation. You cannot achieve what you want alone. Any quarrels now will lead to further problems, so you must be diplomatic and tactful in your communications with friends and colleagues, even if you have to bite your tongue. Being aggressively forceful with your opinions will lose you any ground that you have won; you will have to compromise to get what you want.

Spiritually, the Seven of Swords is advising you to look at your relationship with the land in which you live. The Pagan believes that the land is alive and holy, as is all that dwells upon it—both visible and invisible, the realm of the manifest and the realm of spirit. When this card appears, it is time to develop an awareness of the spiritual dimension of your own environment, whether you live in a city or in the countryside. Modern man has lost the sense of sacredness of place, or only applies it to designated sites, such as churches or historical constructions. All places are special and have their own power and spirit. It is this spirit you should come to know and work with, rather than trying to invoke the spirit of other times and other places.

Reverse Meanings

The Seven of Swords reversed reveals that you have become lazy and indecisive. You can't seem to summon up the energy to finish what you have started and have lost sight of the reason you should. Perhaps you have slipped into doing something you don't really want to do because it was easier than saying no. You need to make an honest assessment of where you stand—this is your life and you must decide what you want and what you don't. You may find it a relief to simply abandon things you have lost interest in.

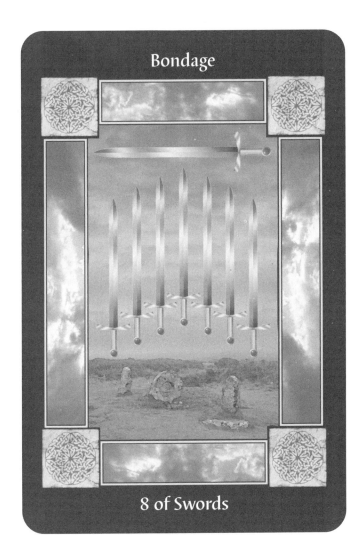

Bondage

8 of Swords

Eight of Swords

The card shows one large sword and seven smaller ones. The background is the Men an Tol in Cornwall.

The Symbolism

In this card there are eight swords. It is easy to get caught up look-ing at the details of the seven small swords and miss the threat of the large one.

The swords hover over the Men an Tol, a Bronze Age monu-ment situated on the Penwith Peninsula in Cornwall. There are four stones in the monument, one fallen, two upright, and a circu-lar holed stone that stands between them. At one time there may have been more to the monument, since more stones are located a short distance away. The stones are aligned to the Beltane and Lughnasa sunrises and the Samhain and Imbolc sunsets. Holed stones, large or small, are emblems of the Goddess, her womb and her power of healing. Children with tuberculosis were passed naked three times though the hole, then drawn three times along the grass widdershins (anti-sunwise). Widdershins is a banishing movement, and so the ritual movement banishes the disease. Crawling into the stone was a ritual act of crawling into the womb of the Goddess and emerging reborn from the other side. Contact with the ground afterward earthed the disease. To the present day, people crawl through the stone widdershins nine times to cure back problems. The stones were also believed to cure barrenness and confer luck on new babies who were passed through the hole. Couples would hold hands through the stone to seal an engage-ment and attract fertility.

If the holed stone represents the womb of the Goddess, then the two uprights are obviously phallic, possibly the twin gods of the summer and winter.

Divinatory Meanings

The Eight of Swords is a card of bondage and restriction, whether the cause of this is an illness, a disability, or family or financial cir-cumstances. You face a difficult choice—it is too late to go back and it seems that to go forward will bring you pain. Any action appears to have unpleasant consequences. However, this dilemma is largely self-created, as the restrictions lie in your own mind: the bondage is your own fear.

The lesson of the Men an Tol in this card is one of healing through letting go. Every human being has restrictions and limitations on what they can do—not everyone can run a marathon, or even walk. Everyone has different talents and abilities and just because you can't do one thing, you don't have to close yourself off to the myriad possibilities that are still obtainable. This card is telling you that it is the bondage to your own fears and self-limitations that needs to be banished.

Reverse Meanings

The Eight of Swords reversed indicates that you can gain temporary relief from your problems by distancing yourself from them, rather than trying to solve them at this time. It may be that this period of respite will enable you to gain a better perspective of what faces you, which may not be as bad as you fear.

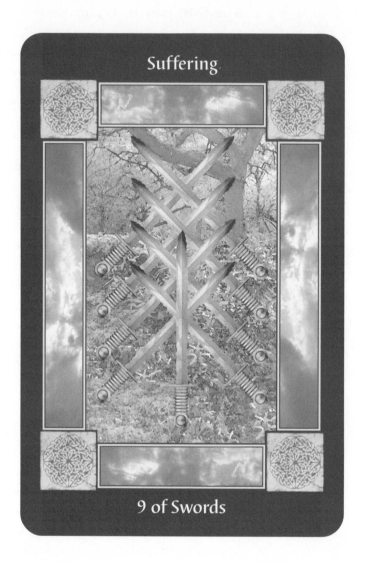

Suffering

9 of Swords

Nine of Swords

The card shows nine rusty swords abandoned in a nettle patch.

The Symbolism

The swords in the picture have been abandoned, probably after some lost battle. They are red with rust. Wild nettles, which will sting anyone who tries to retrieve the weapons, have grown up around them. The nettle has a fierce sting, and may not be picked without paying the price of pain. Though it appears antagonistic, once assimilated it is totally beneficial, full of vitamins and minerals. As such, it teaches the lesson of transmutation.

The nettle is a plant connected to all three realms. It is associated with lightning, and the lightning serpent is said to have imbued the nettle with some of his sting. In ancient lore, the lightning strike is the fertilizing power of the God, which enters the womb of the earth, the Underworld realm where the soul is tempered and transformed. In gypsy belief, the nettle is found growing thickly in spots that mark the subterranean labyrinths that lead to the dwelling places of the earth fairies, to whom the nettle is sacred. Because the nettle is connected to all three realms and the powers of transmutation, it is used in the consecration of the ritual knife.

Divinatory Meanings

The Nine of Swords indicates a time of misfortune that will cause you great pain and unhappiness. What kind of problems you will encounter may be divined from the surrounding cards; they may relate to the end of a relationship, the loss of a loved one, money troubles, or illness. Whatever happens, you will feel oppressed by your troubles. The events indicated by this card can lead to despair and deep depression: any action seems futile, and there seems to be nowhere to turn for help. Your thoughts revolve in fruitless circles and you are tormented by fears of all kinds. You may be plagued by nightmares and evil premonitions.

However, you should bear in mind the lesson of the nettle. It demonstrates that all things have their place in creation, and that those things that appear most unpleasant can be transmuted. It is

those spiritual and life experiences that are most difficult and tax-
ing which are the ones that make you grow most. The swords of
this suit are tempered by fire and this makes them stronger. Direct
action is not indicated at this time, so be patient. Suffering is part
of life and must be worked through to be fully resolved. It is
important to understand the nature of your fears, which may stem
from some event in the past, or some half-shadowed guilt. Everyone has fears of all kinds and it may be that the fear of an event is
worse than the event itself. The anxiety that accompanies the
projected breakup of a relationship—fear of loneliness, rejection,
loss of status—may resolve itself in a new independence and confidence. Loss of possessions may result in a freedom from burdens.
Illness may lead to self-discovery and new perspectives. It all
depends on your approach and attitude.

Reverse Meanings

The Nine of Swords reversed indicates that your fears have
reached hysterical levels and you have lost all sense of proportion.
Mental breakdown is indicated, even suicide. You need the help of
a sympathetic counselor or therapist to help you work through
your problems and put your fears into perspective. There is no
shame in this; sometimes events—whether illness, abuse, or loss—
can cause the subconscious inner demons of the mind to work
overtime and a fresh insight is needed to dissipate them.

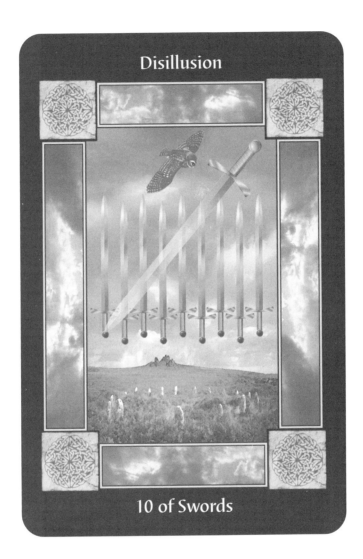

Ten of Swords

The card shows ten swords, one of which disappears and reappears, slashing at the other nine. In the background is Tregaseal Circle and Carn Kenidjack. An owl circles overhead.

The Symbolism

Nine swords are threatened by one larger one, which may or may not be real.

In the background is Carn Kenidjack, a natural stone formation visible from several surrounding prehistoric sites. At the carn, the devil is said to hunt at night for lost souls, while at midnight fights erupt between demons there. Certainly the wind causes the carn to emit a strange low moaning sound which intensifies to a loud hoot. The name *Kenidjack* derives from the ancient Celtic and means "head of the serpent or dragon."

Tregaseal Circle is less than half a mile away. The area is now moor land, and it is widely believed that travelers can be led astray by the piskies or fairy folk on misty evenings. These Little People are the spirits of the barrows and mounds.

An owl flies over the circle. Like most night flying birds, the owl was thought to be a bird of ill omen in many parts of the world. In Britain, the owl call was thought to be a death omen, especially if it was heard during the day or for three nights running. Shakespeare, in *Macbeth*, called the owl "the fatal bellman which gives the stern'st good night."

Owls are very vocal in November, the death time of the year, and then fall silent until February. As such, they are the heralds of the Goddess in her death and winter aspect. They are the servants of the Crone Goddess, and in Scotland the owl is known as Cailleach, which means *hag*.

In the Welsh Mabinogion story of Llew, he is put under a curse by his mother Arianrhod so that he should never marry a mortal woman. His magician uncles Math and Gwydion create for him a bride made from flowers, called Blodeuwedd (*flower-face*). Though she is beautiful and looks like a real woman, she has no heart. She is unfaithful to him and plots to kill him. She is unsuccessful, thanks to Gwydion, and is turned into an owl. Blodeuwedd is a Welsh name for the owl, the face of which some say resembles a flower.

Divinatory Meanings

When the Ten of Swords appears in your spread, it indicates that you are now beginning to see a dream for what it really is—an illusion. Not surprisingly, everything you have built on this illusion is collapsing. Whether this relates to an unrealistic project, a destructive relationship, or a get-rich-quick scheme can be discerned from the surrounding cards. You are deeply disappointed and despairing. At the moment it seems as though there is nothing left, that all hope has been snatched away. However, the way out of the situation lies within yourself. You need to recognize that an inevitable ending has taken place, because what you had was based on a false premise. It is best that it is over, however painful that is. Now you must look to whatever self-deceit or wishful thinking led you to this situation and learn to be more truthful with yourself in the future.

Spiritually, this is the time to be honest with yourself and see through your illusions. Listen to the lessons of the owl. She may be telling you that you need to accept yourself, both light and dark. You need to bring the monsters of your subconscious—your fears, irrational prejudices, and so on—into the light and deal with them. They are blocking your progress and holding you back. The owl is often the familiar of the magician or witch. It speaks of the wisdom that recognizes the dark side—night, winter, the Underworld, old age, and death. These things are a needful balance and are not evil, but part of the cycle of life that must be understood as a whole. This is the realm of the Crone, the Goddess of Wisdom. Owl points the way to true enlightenment, which comes out of the darkness and grows toward the light.

Reverse Meanings

The Ten of Swords reversed heralds a sudden, extreme, and violent change in your life. If you have been involved with untrustworthy people or have been dabbling in shady areas, the advice of this card is to get out now or you will pay a heavy price.

Page of Swords

The card shows a smart young man dressed in yellow. He has light brown hair and blue eyes, and a stern and serious face. His sword lies on the grass beside him. A raven circles in the spring sky above his head, and behind him is a mountain range in Ireland dotted with pine trees. In the foreground are the daffodils of spring.

The Symbolism

Clouds gather above the head of the young Page, who represents the first impulse of the element of air, the power of independent thought.

The raven above his head is often seen circling in storm clouds and it is therefore perceived as a thunderbird. The raven was the messenger of the gods, an informant and guide. It was thought to be the most prophetic of birds, having knowledge of public and private events; people are still spoken of as having "the foresight of a raven." The Celts thought that the outcome of a battle could be foretold by observing ravens, and ravens warned the Irish god Lugh of the invasion of the Formorians. The raven is associated with the Celtic god Bran ("raven"). Bran's head was taken to the White Mount in London, where it continued to prophesy and protect Britain from invasion until King Arthur removed the head as a sign that he was now responsible for protecting Britain. The Tower of London now stands on the site, and Bran's ravens still live there. According to legend, if they ever leave the tower Britain will fall to invaders. Raven is the teacher and protector of seers and clairvoyants.

The Page of Swords is resting in a valley while he contemplates the Spring. Around his feet are yellow daffodils, which represent the powerful regeneration of the earth at this time. Their energy is basic, sexual, instinctive, and vital—the manifestation of magic on the physical plane.

The pine trees of the mountain are another reminder of the season. The pine cone, sometimes called the "tree-egg," is formed in a spiral growth pattern. Because of this, and its phallic shape, it is a symbol of the rebirth and fertility of the Vegetation God. Among the northern Celts, the pine was associated with heroes and warriors, and was one of the chieftain trees of ogham. Though the pine has become popular as a Yule or Christmas tree, this is more properly the fir. The pine is a tree of the spring equinox and the return of the Vegetation God. Images of vegetation gods are often made from pine as they are seen as containing His spirit.

Divinatory Meanings

In this card we encounter the first impulse of the powers of air—the beginning of independent thinking, rather than accepting the ideas of others. This mental capacity does not leap into being fully formed, but must be developed.

All of the court cards can represent actual people who are influencing your life. The Page of Swords may appear as a young man (or woman) with a sharp, analytical mind, eternally curious and always trying to get to the bottom of a situation or person. Once he has, he will get bored and move on to the next mystery. The Page of Swords is a rather detached and impersonal individual who likes to be surrounded by people, but rarely gets close to any of them: he hates to feel pinned down and commitment is not a word he likes. He rarely involves himself with grand causes, but lives by his own set of ethics, which might be quite revolutionary. No amount of argument or logical persuasion will shake him loose from them. He is a visionary with his own ideas, and practical matters do not interest him very much. Though he is always polite and kind, he may sometimes try to shock people, just to see their reactions. He has a sharp mind and misses very little. He is very useful to have on your side, but in opposition he hates to lose and is capable of using all the tricks in the book to win.

Thought is a powerful force and it may be that you need to utilize your analytical skills to develop your own ideas rather than merely accepting those of others.

Reverse Meanings

Depending on the surrounding cards, the Page of Swords reversed can indicate ill health or other unforeseen events that will cause changes to your plans.

The Page of Swords reversed is warning you to beware of a deceitful person who is not what he seems, he is two-faced and you are only seeing one of them! He is motivated by envy and vindictiveness, and given the chance he will betray you.

Knight of Swords

In this card, a knight clad in golden armor carries a sword before him. In the background is a stormy sky over a mountainous region.

The Symbolism

The knight of this card is a capable young man, well used to combat. Ready for any eventuality, he carries his sword before him as he strides confidently over the terrain. He is on his latest quest, and as soon as he has completed this one, he will look for another. He hates to be still.

The sky in the picture is stormy and demonstrates the nature of the element of air, always in motion, always changing.

Divinatory Meanings

Air is a changeable element, and this card indicates that you must be prepared for sudden changes that temporarily throw your life into chaos. This may be because a new idea or vision throws you off your planned course although, depending on surrounding cards, it can be the result of a sudden illness, accident, or surgical operation.

The Knight of Swords may indicate the influence of an actual person who will initiate changes in your life. The Knight is a mercurial man with extreme, but changeable, opinions. What he fiercely believes one day may be radically altered the next. He is clever and idealistic and loves to examine new ideas and new horizons, but lacks the persistence to fully pursue them. He gets bored very quickly and needs constant stimulation and excitement and will move from one thing to another in a short space of time. However, he is quite charming and very good with words; he can probably talk you into anything. He could be a writer or a salesman. He abounds with nervous energy and is very impatient with people who are indecisive.

It may be that you need something of the spirit of the Knight of Swords. You know that you have something that you have always wanted to do, whether it is a special trip, a career change, or a creative project that you have been putting off. Stop vacillating and do something positive. It may just turn out to be the most rewarding thing you have ever done.

Reverse Meanings

The Knight of Swords reversed is warning you to beware of a clever liar who is deceitful and sly. He likes to provoke quarrels and may be maneuvering you into a tricky situation.

Imagination

Queen of Swords

Queen of Swords

The card shows a handsome young woman with light brown hair and gray eyes. Her expression is benign but serious. She holds aloft a sword and is dressed in drifting yellow robes. It is the spring equinox—when the earth regenerates—and the land around her is beginning to blossom with spring flowers including primroses and gorse, through which bees buzz. Behind her are silver birch trees and a hare appears at her feet.

The Symbolism

The card shows the young Maiden of Spring whose regenerative powers bring life back to the earth after winter. She presides over the gifts of imagination and the inspiration of poets.

The trees in the background are birches. Magically, their vibration is the power of new beginnings, of leaving behind the winter and negativity, cleansing and purification in preparation for the summer, and new creative opportunities. The white trunk of the birch represents the shining light of purity and freshness. Birch rods are used in country ritual for driving out the old year.

At the spring equinox, the Celtic Druids would collect the sap of the birch to make it into wine to celebrate the coming of spring and to release the spirit of the tree to give strength to the waxing sun so that it might give its power to the new growing season, when the light begins to gain on the dark.

Also shown is the gorse, one of the earliest shrubs to flower in the spring. Its yellow blossoms provide one of the first foods for the bees. The importance of the gorse to our ancestors is indicated by the fact that it is ranked as a chieftain tree in the ogham alphabet, where it is called *onn*, one of the "cauldron of five trees," the vowels of the ogham alphabet. It is sacred to the Spring Goddess and her hare totem often finds shelter beneath it.

Hares were sacred to the ancient British. Killing and eating the hare was taboo, and the penalty for doing so was to be struck with cowardice. The Celts lifted the restriction on hunting the hare at the spring equinox and made a ritual hunt and consumption. The Anglo-Saxons also venerated the hare, and a ritual hare hunt was a feature of the spring festival of the goddess Eostre. Folk survivals of these rituals still exist. The hare is associated with the east, the station of light-bringing and resurrected vegetation gods, the dawn, and the vernal equinox. The Teutonic goddess Eostre is often depicted as hare-headed. Her hare laid the egg of new life to herald the rebirth of the year, and even now the Easter bunny is said to distribute eggs in springtime. Eostre's name is preserved in *Easter*.

At the young Maiden's feet grow primroses, a plant much prized by the Druids and connected with the Spring Goddess in Welsh Druidic magic. The poem *The Chair of Taliesin* describes the initiation of a bard with a drink made from primrose and vervain, which gave poetic inspiration.

Feeding on the gorse nectar are bees, creatures symbolic of both regeneration and inspiration. A very old belief states that bees were born in the body of dead animals, and so they were seen as symbols of rebirth—new life coming from death. Even now you find bees carved on tombstones.

Bees were sometimes called the "birds of the muses," bringers of divine inspiration and bestowers of eloquence and honeyed words. Legends surrounding ancient poets and orators often tell of a swarm of bees alighted on their mouths as babies, giving them the gift of sweet words. The honey bee orients itself on its journey by the angle and position of the sun, and the Celts regarded it as a messenger that traveled the paths of sunlight to the realm of the spirits.

Divinatory Meanings

This card falls under the influence of the Spring Goddess, who brings rebirth to the vegetation cycle of the earth. It is also the card of bards and poets.

The power of the Queen of Swords is the power of imagination and positive thought; it is through your thought patterns that you create your vision of your past, view your present, and envision the future. The way you think about things shapes what they are. The ability of imagination and positive thought to bring things into being is one of the first principles of magic.

It is time to look forward and use the powerful creative energies that surround you to forge your future. Now is not the time to delay or make excuses for inaction, but to think positively and use your imagination. The hare is touched by a divine madness in the spring, dancing and boxing. Theirs is the anarchy that overturns dogmatic tradition and restrictions and brings new ideas and inspirations. Hare may be telling you that this is the time to break free of restrictions and be unconventional. This can be a time of great energy and creativity, with inspiration coming from unexpected sources. This message is reinforced by Bee, heralding a time of great creativity or spiritual progress. This card is particularly fortuitous for poets and bards, as it brings the sweet honey of true words.

The appearance of the Queen of Swords in your spread may indicate that a woman will become important in your life. She is graceful and unconventional, quick-witted and confident. Though she likes to be with people, to talk to them and listen to them in equal measure, she is not happy in a crowd. She is artistic and loves music, poetry, and beautiful things. The Queen of Swords is totally honest and a seeker after truth, hating ignorant prejudice and blind faith. She sees beneath the surface of things and has an intense desire to see justice and fair play. She is adept at balancing opposing factions to further her desires. Her nobility of mind can often mean that she is lonely; she is loyal and has the highest ideals, others often disappoint her by not measuring up. Any man she gets involved with had better be perfect, any less will not do for her rarefied ideal. She can appear cold and proud, because her intellect and ideals are more important to her than any physical attraction. Be warned—she is repelled by excessive displays of emotion and hates anyone telling her what she should do and how she should behave.

Reverse Meanings

You have the habit of looking at life in a negative way. You don't even enjoy the good things that come to you because you are too busy looking for the catch. You are missing out on opportunities and letting life pass you by. Remember the hare—he is telling you that you need to loosen up and stop being so dogmatic; you are blocking any progress you might make with your attitudes.

It may be that you need to consider the needs of others in your circle and stop thinking only of yourself, as selfishness may destroy the whole enterprise. Do not be unrealistic in your demands of other people, it will create problems. If you do not take heed, you will find yourself isolated and feel betrayed, though you will have brought it on yourself.

You need the magic of the gorse: its lesson is one of hope. The Elder People used to make a cleansing tea of the early flowers to purify them after the winter and prepare the body and the spirit for the energizing influence of spring. It is time to re-examine some of your most cherished ideas and evaluate whether they really help you grow, or whether you are hiding behind them. Your quest is to rediscover your true Self, to reconnect with your soul and find your real purpose. You have lost yourself somewhere along the way. This card indicates that you now have the opportunity to let go of your negative thought patterns and cleanse yourself of bitterness, to discover within yourself the energy and personal strength needed to take positive action.

The Queen of Swords reversed may indicate the appearance of a woman in your life. She has suffered great loss and is possibly a widow. Her experiences have made her hard and bitter beneath an attractive surface. She may be quick to take offense and you will only know this when it rebounds on you. She can be cruel and deceitful, she loves gossip—particularly rumors of a malicious kind. She is narrow-minded, intolerant of any views other than those that coincide with her own, and makes a very bad enemy.

King of Swords

The card shows the King of Swords as a handsome young man. He has fine, intelligent features, dark brown hair and eyes. He is seated on a golden throne in the open air, his yellow garments flutter in the breeze. The wind also stirs the clouds above his head and supports a hovering crane. The vernal equinox sun rises over the mountainous background and an alder tree can be seen growing from a crag. At the King's feet, a snake slithers through flowering bistort and tansy.

The Symbolism

The King of Swords is Lord of the Powers of Air. Magically, air rules all mental activity from the inception of an idea to the gathering of knowledge. Air is also the power of the communication of ideas and knowledge through sound, vocalization, music, and writing. Air corresponds to the magical tool of the sword, the season of spring and the dawn. It is associated with the direction of the east and the festival of the vernal equinox, Ostara, when new life gestates and grows with the increase of light and warmth. Air is inspiration, the breath of life; it moves and changes constantly. It can be the cooling breeze or the destructive hurricane.

The King is strong and dynamic, intelligent and calculating. His familiar is the crane, which is connected in mythology to gods and goddesses who preside over the mysteries of regeneration and reincarnation. There is an ancient association between long-necked birds and the sun. Cranes and herons standing by the waters are said to be the first birds to greet the dawn. They catch many small fish to feed their young and have the curious habit of laying them on the bank, tails together, in the form of a wheel. The wheel is the symbol of the sun and its passage through the year.

The Celtic god Ogma is said to have invented the ogham alphabet after seeing the flight of cranes. Crane keeps the secrets of magical writing. The Druids kept their ogham lots in a crane bag. For our ancestors, the act of writing was far removed from what it is today. To write a character was to connect with the thing that character represented and to call it into being. Many early alphabets were angular in appearance, since they had to be carved into stone or scratched onto bark. The legs of the crane in flight are said to resemble these characters.

For the Druids, crane knowledge referred to secrets of the ogham alphabet and all that it entailed. Each character was assigned a tree, plant, animal, bird, and color, each embodying a wealth of lore and learning. The Irish sea god Manannan owned a magical bag made from crane skin. It contained several treasures— the shears of the king of Scotland, the helmet of the king of Lochlainn, the bones from Assails' swine, the hook of the smith Goibne, a shirt, and a strip from the back of the great whale. These were the vowels of the ogham alphabet, and the strip of the whale represented the horizon (the sea was called "the whale road"), the stave on which ogham was written.

Crane is often the familiar of poets and bards, conveying them on Otherworldly journeys to the realms of divine inspiration. Crane is an intermediary between the gods and humankind and brings teachings from the Upperworld.

At the feet of the King grows tansy and bistort. The common name of tansy is thought to come from the Greek word *athanatos*, which means *immortal*. A traditional use of the herb was in tansy pudding, a rich custardy dessert or in a bread or dough cake, called tansy cake, which was eaten at Easter. Tansy celebrates the renewal of the God at Ostara and is employed in incenses, added to the cup, or used in the festival food. Bistort is a power plant of the vernal equinox. Its roots are twisted and serpentine and it is sometimes called "the English serpent tree," associated with another equinox totem, the snake.

The serpent lives in the Underworld and emerges from it to shed its skin and be reborn anew. As such, it is a symbol of rebirth and the wholeness of the cycle. At the equinox, the Druids celebrated the mystery of the serpent's egg, laid by the Goddess and split open by the Sun God.

Divinatory Meanings

The King of Swords is the personification of the powers of the element of air, Lord of Gorias, the mystical city of the east.

The King of Swords calls upon you to develop within yourself the qualities of the element of air, especially your mental powers, the intellectual capacity of developing strategies to make the changes you want. You have had some inspired and innovative ideas and it is time to move decisively and put them into action yourself; do not wait for others to do it for you. Demonstrate the qualities of leadership and others will follow.

The King's familiar is the crane, which speaks of teaching and of knowledge passed on. Knowledge does no good sitting in a dusty cupboard, it should be circulated and shared. However, Crane also speaks of guarding knowledge from those who would misuse it, so be careful whom you speak to. Crane may be telling you that you might find answers in something you are reading, or that you will find value in writing, either making things clearer to yourself or passing on what you have learned.

When the card of the King of Swords appears in your spread, it can indicate that a mature man is about to be influential in your life. He has very high moral ideals and is an intellectual; he does not allow his heart to rule his head. He has formulated his own rules and doesn't admit exceptions to them based on individual circumstance. Because of this he can seem cold and hard. The King of Swords is a charismatic leader with great personal strength and dynamism. He is capable of instigating great changes around himself.

Reverse Meanings

When the King of Swords appears reversed in your spread, he is telling you that you have too much air in your makeup. For you the intellect and the idea are all important, not the application of them. Because of this, very few of your ideas become realized and they are ultimately wasted. You need to develop the other elements in equal balance to realize your full potential.

The reversed card may be warning you to beware of an obstinate man of impersonal and calculating temperament who can be sometimes cruel, unjust, and malicious.

Suit of Wands

Element: fire

Season: summer
Beltane to Lughnasa Eve

Color: red

Attributes: the spirit, the will,
creativity, career, vision

Direction: south

Festival: Coamhain

Ace of Wands

The card depicts a large oaken wand. Though it has been cut from the tree, it still bursts with life and greenery grows from it. Energy radiates from it. In the dawn light is Lanyon Quoit, Cornwall, England.

The Symbolism

The Ace of Wands is the root of the powers of fire. The wand is the magical tool of the south and appears in various guises as the staff, the arrow, and the spear. It comes from the magical city of the south, Finias.

The suit of wands corresponds to the element of fire, the season of summer, noon, and the direction of the south. Its station on the wheel is the midsummer solstice, which we call Coamhain, when the earth flowers and grows lush in the heat.

Magically, fire rules creativity, life energy, and the spirit. Fire is the illumination within, the force of the spirit. It is the glow of the candle flame, the warmth of the hearth, the burning heat of the desert, the incandescence of the sun—the fire that both purifies and destroys. Fire is the power of inner sight and creative vision, directing it and controlling it to make it manifest in the world.

In this card, the wand is shown against the background of Lanyon Quoit, which stands amid moorland in Cornwall, a prehistoric burial chamber at least 5,000 years old. It is sometimes called the Giant's Quoit or the Giant's Table and is linked by a ley to the Tregaseal Stone Circle, the Carfury Standing Stone, Chysauster prehistoric village, and a stone cross at Brunion. Formerly, there was a ring of stones a hundred yards to the north, another barrow and ring to the southwest, and a "high stone" that once stood eighty yards away to the west northwest. The capstone supposedly fell off during a severe storm in the early 1800s (more likely it had been weakened by treasure hunters) and was erected again ten years later—some feat, as it weighs thirteen and a half tons. The quoit is part of a long mound, and originally it probably had an ante-chamber and an inner room.

Quoits (sometimes called *dolmens* or *cromlechs*) are among the oldest prehistoric structures. They were oriented to specific solar or lunar events and were very visible in the landscape. Quoits are usually described as graves, though bones are rarely found inside. We know that people were not buried there and then the tomb sealed, like a pyramid, but that they instead continued to be used by the living for up to a thousand years. The people of the tribe went to the mounds to consult the spirits of the ancestors, to bring them gifts, undergo initiations, and perform rituals to include the ancestors in the continuing cycle of nature—life, marriage, death, and rebirth.

Divinatory Meanings

Aces always represent powerful bursts of raw energy. The Ace of Wands appearing in your spread indicates a powerful new cycle of creative energy and inspiration. This is a power available to everyone, not just the artist, writer, or musician.

The energy of the Ace of Wands usually manifests as a general feeling of restlessness and dissatisfaction with things as they are. You feel that new and better things are possible; though you are not quite sure what they are, you feel impelled to pursue them. This card is advising you to trust your vision, however silly your ideas may seem, because your life is about to open up.

Depending on surrounding cards, this creativity can manifest as works of art, writing, or music; the founding of a business; or even a family.

Reverse Meanings

When the Ace of Wands appears reversed in your spread, it is telling you that you are not giving reign to your creative potential; you have plenty of ideas but you do not see them through. You need to learn to have more confidence in yourself and your creative vision. Make a resolution to finish the things you start and you will surprise yourself and the people around you with your talent.

Depending on the surrounding cards, the Ace of Wands reversed can indicate problems of a sexual nature—frigidity or impotence. This, too, is a denial of personal expression and you need to look at the reasons this situation has arisen and seek help in resolving it. Sometimes this card can mean the inability to conceive a child.

Courage

2 of Wands

Two of Wands

The card shows the chalk hill figure of the Long Man of Wilmington, who holds a long staff in either hand.

The Symbolism

The long Man of Wilmington is in Sussex, one of the last areas to become Christianized. He is a 230-foot-high chalk figure carved into the turf of Windover Hill and is said to be the largest drawing of a human figure in the world. By the middle of the nineteenth century he had become so overgrown by grass and weeds that he was only visible in certain lights and after snow; the Duke of Devonshire paid for his restoration. According to tradition he once had a hat, and evidence suggests this may have been a horned helmet. In each hand he holds a staff. It may be that the giant is positioned on the hill so that he is only visible when the sun strikes him at a certain angle, and the position of his staves alters with the position of the sun.

Locally, he is called "the Green Man." It is thought that he may have been carved by the the Atrebates, an Iron Age Celtic tribe, and represents a guardian tribal god, though some think it more likely he portrays a later Saxon god or folk hero. His precise identity remains elusive. *The Doomsday Book* records the area where he lies as "Wandelmestrei," named after the Germanic God Waendal. Another possibility is that he is "the fighting man," the badge of King Harold, the last of the Saxon Kings.

In folklore tales, the giant was once a living person who battled with another giant. They fought by throwing huge boulders at each other. Eventually the Long Man was killed and laid out on the hill, where his outline remains.

Divinatory Meanings

The Two of Wands calls on you to become something of an intellectual warrior armed with the courage of your convictions. Your ideas have a lot of potential, but you will need to work hard to bring them to fruition. You will need a lot of willpower and dedication to follow your vision. This is not without risk, but if you choose cozy but boring security, you will never have the chance to know what you are really capable of.

Reverse Meanings

When the Two of Wands appears reversed in your spread, it indicates that you are tempted to use unscrupulous means to achieve your ambitions or gain money, despite the fact that this would be a betrayal of your principles and might hurt people dear to you. Be warned that you will derive no pleasure from things achieved in this manner, you will lose the respect and friendship of others. Moreover, you will feel that you have let yourself down and proved yourself unworthy in your own estimation.

Foundation

3 of Wands

Three of Wands

The card shows three flowering rods in late summer against the background of a cornfield. Strawberries grow on them.

The Symbolism

The three rods, which represent creative ideas, were planted in the ground and have now begun to blossom and fruit. They seem to promise a good harvest and are shown against the background of a ripe summer day and a cornfield just turning gold.

The fruits depicted are strawberries, sacred to the Summer Mother Goddess and offered to her at midsummer rituals. As such, they appear in folk magic as talismans for pregnant women, carried to ensure a safe delivery.

Strawberries are also attractive to the fairy wildfolk and are left as offerings to them to solicit blessings on the harvest and the milk yield.

Divinatory Meanings

The Three of Wands indicates that you are entitled to celebrate the initial success of a project. Things have gone well so far, and you were lucky enough to be in the right place at the right time. However, though the foundations have been well laid, you will now need to put in a lot of hard work and creative energy. Be flexible, as it may become necessary to modify or improve the original idea. This can be an exciting period when you will be stretched and challenged and will achieve more than you ever thought possible.

Depending on the surrounding cards, the Three of Wands can mean that a long engagement to one person will suddenly end, to be followed by a swiftly arranged marriage to another.

Reverse Meanings

The Three of Wands reversed indicates that a venture that looked promising fails, causing you disappointment. Through misguided pride, you refuse help when you need it. Stop being so obstinate and admit that you need other people sometimes.

Development

4 of Wands

Four of Wands

The card shows four wands within a circle, making a spinning wheel.

The Symbolism

The four wands of this card join together to form an eight-pointed wheel, which spins. This is the symbol of the ever-turning seasons—from seeding to harvest to seeding again—in the Eternal Return. The eight points represent the eight major festivals of the Pagan year.

Divinatory Meanings

The Four of Wands indicates that you have put a lot of hard work into a project and are now starting to reap the rewards. You have earned a rest but will soon have to start work again. However, you should be wary of rushing things, pay attention to detail, and make sure you have enough support and financial backing to see things through to completion.

On a personal level, this card indicates that the demands of a relationship will ease off and will become more happy and harmonious. For the unattached, romance is in the air.

Reverse Meanings

The Four of Wands reversed in your spread indicates that though the completion of a project is delayed by various obstacles, there is no need to worry as it will soon come to a successful completion.

Five of Wands

The card shows five sharp spears. In the background is the mountainous landscape of Glendalough, Ireland, in summer.

The Symbolism

The five spears of the picture seem to point toward the mountain tops. They hover above the ground, not touching it. They represent aspirations out of touch with the earth or reality.

Symbolically, the mountain is the model of the universe and represents the aspiration of the soul, with the spirit at the summit. It was often the custom for seers and poets to climb mountains in search of communion with the gods and to gain inspiration from being apart from the world of men. However, these enlightened people would then bring their wisdom down from the mountain top to share with their tribe and use it to help improve their lives.

Divinatory Meanings

The Five of Wands indicates that you are in danger of becoming carried away in following a dream and not noticing what is actually going on around you—reality is about to intrude. It may be that you do not have the skills or financial backing to achieve what you want and will have to compromise your high-flown ideas for something more realistic. It may be that your head has been in the clouds and you have not noticed that the bills are mounting up, that necessary work has been neglected, and that your family and friends resent being ignored. You are being rather selfish and things are starting to fall apart even if you haven't noticed it yet. To manifest your dream you must be more realistic and keep your feet firmly on the ground. Unless you start to pay attention, you will face serious problems with money and may lose what you have, including those you love.

Spiritually, this card indicates that you are ungrounded, getting carried away in a selfish fashion with ideas and visions, and neglecting to also act in the material world. You are ignoring mundane matters that need to be attended to and ignoring people who need you. This is a serious lack of balance and is in no way real spiritual progress. You live in the manifest world and must relate to it and achieve a harmony between the needs of the mind, the body, and the spirit. Any neglect of one will lead to a harming of the others, and ultimately to illness and depression.

Reverse Meanings

The Five of Wands reversed indicates that you seem to be angry with the world in general, provoking unnecessary arguments, making cutting remarks, and indulging in compulsive and unnecessary competition with others. You are hurting inside and you are trying to hurt others. You need to recognize that this is not going to heal your pain or make you any friends. You must confront the real reason for your anger and take steps to deal with it.

Six of Wands

The card shows six spears resting peacefully and tied with a victory garland. The background is an Iron Age fort in Gloucestershire, England. Swallows flit through the summer sky.

The Symbolism

The six spears of this card have finished with battle; the fight has been won. They are no longer needed and lie tied up with a garland in token of victory. Their owners have left the battlefield to go back to their homes and families, confident that the conflict is over. The remains of the fort lie in the peaceful summer sunshine and the swallow, the emblem of joy, flies above it.

Throughout the summer, the twittering, warbling song of the swallow is heard from dawn until sunset. The birds sing while perched or in flight, gracefully swooping up and down. Swallows are summer visitors all over Britain, appearing at the beginning of March and leaving in October. They are associated with the transformation of the land in spring, heralding the coming of the gentle rains that fertilize the earth.

The swallow is said to have brought fire to humankind from the Underworld, and burned itself in the process, accounting for its red throat and smoke-blue wings. Because of their association with fire, it was thought that swallows nesting beneath the eaves of a house would offer it protection from lightning, fire, and storms.

Omens were also taken from the behavior of swallows: it is bad luck if the swallow deserts its nest; if a swallow is disturbed it means a bad harvest; to see swallows fighting is a bad omen; if a swallow flies into a house it brings joy with it.

Divinatory Meanings

The Six of Wands is a good news card and indicates that, after a lot of hard work and difficulties, you are now beginning to achieve the success you dreamed of—one that is recognized by other people. This can mean that you have gained some qualifications, a promotion at work, have won a race you trained for, had an exhibition of your paintings, or have performed your music in public to general acclaim.

The fire of the swallow is the hearth fire that lies at the center of the home. It provides warmth, comfort, and the means of preparing food. The swallow heralds a time of domestic harmony and stability.

On a spiritual level, for our ancestors the hearth fire was also the *axis mundi* of the house, through which the spirits could travel to the Otherworld. The fire of the swallow is not the fire that burns and consumes, but the flame that warms and nurtures the spirit. Swallow teaches the lesson of the transformation of the spirit by fire and can lead you into the realms of pure joy, for though the spirit must sometimes be tempered by hardship, it must also be kindled by ecstasy.

Reverse Meanings

The Six of Wands reversed in your spread indicates that you will receive some bad news. Perhaps a rival is promoted over you, or your projects are delayed by red tape. Take comfort in the lesson of the swallow: pleasure and happiness will come from your home and family; it is time to appreciate these. You should make an effort to settle quarrels within your home and to not waste time and energy in petty disputes. Make an effort to understand the need of those close to you to grow and change. Allow yourself to be happy.

Rivalry

7 of Wands

Seven of Wands

The card shows six spears stacked peacefully on the ground, but the large club of the Cerne Abbas Giant threatens them.

The Symbolism

The seventh wand of this card is the large club of the Cerne Abbas Giant, which threatens the six spears before it.

The Cerne Abbas Giant is a 180-foot chalk hill figure in Dorset, who brandishes a hundred-foot-long club above his head. His origins are unknown, though in folklore tradition he was a sheep thief who was murdered by the local villagers who commemorated his demise by cutting his outline in the turf of the hill. He is almost certainly a fertility god for obvious reasons! Because of this, many customs grew up around him: barren women would sit on him to be cured, girls would pray at his feet that they would not die a spinster, and couples had intercourse on the hill to ensure conception. On May Day, a maypole used to be erected above his head in an earthwork called the Trendle, or the Frying Pan. He may have been a local Pagan God called Helith or Heil or Helis, possibly an incarnation of Hercules, whose worship the Romans brought to Britain. However, the name of the place, Cerne Abbas, is from the Celtic river Cerne, possibly a deity, and *abbas*, which means *abbey*, since there is an abbey, which was founded in the tenth century, nearby. There is also a holy well at the foot of the hill.

He is probably a tribal god who protects the land. The fertility traditions continue—May Day Morris dancing has been revived and women continue to visit the giant in search of fertility.

Divinatory Meanings

The Seven of Wands indicates that you will face stiff competition in the area of creative endeavors or business projects. You will have to reach new levels of imagination and creativity to get your ideas accepted in the face of envious rivals. This is best accomplished by being firm but diplomatic if you want people to listen to your ideas and accept them.

However, the Cerne Abbas Giant is a fertility figure and heralds the flow of creativity. Depending on the surrounding cards, you may be about to embark on a course of study or take up a new career as a writer or teacher.

212 Minor Arcana • Wands

Reverse Meanings

The Seven of Wands reversed indicates that you are losing opportunities through indecisiveness, or that you are too ready to give
up in the face of opposition when, with just a little more effort,
you would win. Are you really so timid, or are you actually avoiding success through fear of responsibility?

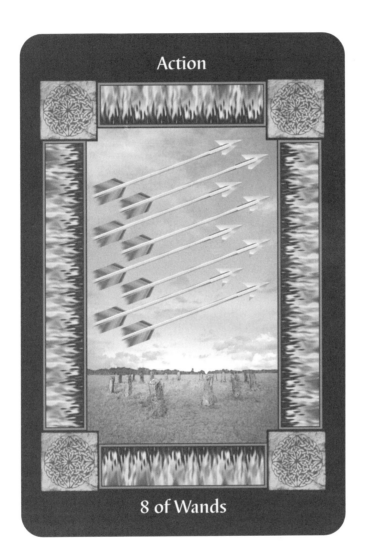

Eight of Wands

The card shows eight feathered arrows flying swiftly through the air. In the background is the Merry Maidens stone circle in Cornwall, England.

The Symbolism

The Merry Maidens is a stone circle standing on the Penwith Peninsula of Cornwall consisting of nineteen evenly spaced stones. According to local legend, they are young girls tuned to stone for the sin of dancing on the Sabbath. Nearby are two granite pillars called the Pipers, said to be the two evil spirits who tempted the maidens. The legend is a fairly late one, and the two pillars may have originally represented the twin aspects of the Sun God. The circle is surrounded by a number of other prehistoric sites and it is thought that a second circle once stood 400 yards to the southwest.

In this card, eight arrows fly above the circle. The many flint arrowheads that are found around Britain, known as elf bolts, were believed to be the fairy arrows of the Little People, the people of the mounds. Bows and arrows had religious significance.

Many gods and goddesses throughout the world are portrayed as hunters, armed with bows and arrows. The god of love fires his arrows of love, moon goddesses have crescent-moon-shaped bows, and Sagittarius, the Archer, ends the year before the sun is reborn in the house of Capricorn. The rays of the sun are described as arrow shafts, and moon beams as the arrows of the moon.

Robin Hood, the forest spirit, hunted with a long bow. At his death, he is reputed to have called for his bow and fired an arrow, asking to be buried where the arrow landed.

The longbow was the traditional weapon of the English, as opposed to the crossbow of the Norman oppressors. Though the crossbow is a more powerful weapon, the longbow is more silent, a definite aid to poachers and freedom fighters. When the Normans invaded, they made the forests the preserves of the nobility, preventing the regular hunting of winter game that the population had relied on. The longbow in skilled hands was able to kill a fully armored knight. At the battle of Agincout, the Saxon peasantry with their longbows defeated the French knights, and in the Middle Ages it became compulsory for every male over seven to possess a longbow his own height and to practice with it for several hours a week.

Divinatory Meanings

The Eight of Wands marks the end of a period of inactivity and indicates that this is the time to be up and doing things. Your imagination will now flow freely, and any creative blocks you have experienced will be broken through. Things will now go smoothly for you and you will be able to make rapid progress.

The arrows may indicate that a message or a letter arrives that will call for a quick response, perhaps necessitating a journey.

The Eight of Wands is often called the arrows of love, and romance is in the air. Be bold and seize the opportunity.

Reverse Meanings

The Eight of Wands reversed indicates that you have done something very foolish on impulse. Unfortunately, this is going to have some far-reaching consequences. You will receive some bad news and, according to surrounding cards, may even be in danger of losing your job.

If you have plans to travel, be prepared for unexpected delays and cancellations.

Nine of Wands

The card depicts a fence made from nine rods against the background of Edale in Derbyshire, England.

The Symbolism

The card shows a defensive barrier constructed from the nine wands of the human will. It is erected on top of a hill in Edale, which is said to be haunted by phantom horses and phantom dogs. The position is unassailable, with a clear view of the surrounding countryside.

The foreground of the hill is covered in heather, which grows freely in the mountains. It was an important plant to the Celts, who dignified it by classifying it as one of the ogham trees, *ura*. It teaches the lesson of overcoming the ego and how to empathize and work with others; it teaches of one's place in the web of being. It is a plant connected with Otherworld travel and helps on the outward spiral of initiation, when the spirit is regenerated and returns to the world. The Picts brewed a legendary ale from heather and refused to divulge the secret to the Norse invaders, even under torture. Heather is placed at the south on the wheel, the festival of midsummer when the God comes into his full powers.

Divinatory Meanings

Just when you think that you have exhausted all your reserves of strength and you are tired and despairing, feeling you can take no more, from somewhere you find a last gasp of energy and triumph against all the odds. Put your faith in the resilience of your inner spirit.

This card can indicate recovery from a debilitating illness or release from a frightening and worrying situation. This card is telling you to be strong, then nothing and no one will be able to drag you down.

Reverse Meanings

Your obstinacy and refusal to compromise has put you in the position of having to defend something that is really indefensible. Unless you can show some strength of character and admit you are wrong, you stand to lose a lot more than you imagine.

Depending on the surrounding cards, the Nine of Wands reversed can indicate ill health.

Ten of Wands

Five iron wands oppose five bronze wands. In the background is Wayland's Smithy, a chambered Neolithic long barrow in Berkshire, England.

The Symbolism

Wayland's Smithy is located only about a mile from the Uffington Horse, a chalk hill figure. Wayland, or Volund, was a Saxon smith god, and it is said that if a horse should be tethered at Wayland's Smithy under a full moon, the owner returning in the morning would find it newly shod. The Smithy is actually a burial chamber, an Underworld womb of the Goddess where the ancients believed that the dead prepared for rebirth. Wayland was an incarnation of the Underworld smith who tempered the spirit on its journey through the Underworld to prepare it for new life.

The horseshoe, with its crescent moon shape, represents the lunar goddess. It equates the horns of power and protection with the receptive cup and nourishment. Horseshoes were nailed above doors to protect the threshold, a dividing line between two places and therefore vulnerable. The iron had power over the fairy folk, witches, and spirits, and the crescent shape symbolized the Goddess, fertility, and the rebirth of the midwinter sun through the horns of the moon.

Blacksmiths were akin to magicians; working with metals was a magical process. The ore had to be mined from the womb of Mother Earth, then the metal extracted by the power of fire, the little brother of the sun. Bronze is composed of copper and tin, the red copper symbolizing the Goddess as fertile mother and the white tin the virgin. The red and the white also symbolize the sun and moon. The coming of the Iron Age was something of a technical revolution. Iron is a much stronger metal than bronze, and people with iron weapons soon defeated those with bronze. Iron weapons were therefore seen as having power over the deities and spirits associated with bronze.

Divinatory Meanings

You have taken on far too many commitments, and a sense of oppression weighs you down. Perhaps you are running a business that takes up every moment of your time, doing too much overtime at work, or just have too many things going on at once. You are certainly not enjoying yourself and you feel very overburdened. Any excitement or satisfaction that you once had in your enterprise has been stifled, and you have no time or energy for personal creativity and pleasure. You must relinquish some of your self-imposed responsibilities to achieve any of your goals; learn to delegate and leave things that don't really need doing alone.

The Ten of Wands demonstrates the use of pure brute force, detached from any spiritual or moral reason. This card can indicate that, if you are working magically, you want results and effects without understanding or purpose, unleashing destructive forces that will rebound on you.

Reverse Meanings

You are playing the martyr, taking on responsibilities and doing things that could easily be accomplished by others so that you can show how burdened you are. You are envious of those around you and intent on spoiling their pleasure by spreading malicious gossip. It's too bad they can all see straight through your schemes. If you don't stop, you are going to end up very lonely.

Page of Wands

A young man dressed in a yellow tunic and a red cloak holds a flaming torch as he crouches before a small fire on a summer night. He has red hair and blue eyes. Celandines grow at his feet and two dragonflies hover in the air.

The Symbolism

The Page of Wands represents the first impulse of the element of fire, its tentative glimmering of light. He is dressed in flame-colored clothes of saffron and red. He has just lit a torch from the small fire at his feet. With it he sees a little way through the darkness that surrounds him.

It is a warm summer evening and celandines, dedicated to the sun god Bel, grow at the feet of the young man. Fire is the little brother of the sun, and legends tell that humankind stole the divine force of the sun to warm their hearths and illuminate their spirits.

The dragonflies that fly in the twilight are power animals of high summer, sometimes called "the adders of the air" or "the snake's servants." They are said to have a magical relationship with adders and hover near them, though their real relationship is with the serpent or dragon power of the land. They are considered to be very lucky, and when country people see them, they make a wish.

Divinatory Meanings

The Page of Wands indicates that you have creative potential that is as yet undeveloped. While your efforts may presently be clumsy and immature, this card is telling you that your talent is worth nurturing. Only with time, practice, and experience can your abilities be developed, so do not let others deter you because your first results are not all you would like them to be.

Like all of the court cards, the Page of Wands can indicate a real person who will be influential in your life. The Page is a young man or woman who is rather arrogant and egotistical. The Page likes to be the center of attention, and often is because he is attractive, graceful, and fun loving. He dresses well and rather theatrically and his ideas are original and creative. The Page is warmhearted and makes a very good friend—if you can put up with him condescendingly telling you how to live your life when his own is a mess. Remember that he responds best to flattery, and he is easily hurt. He makes a very bad enemy. Whatever you do, don't fall in love with him if he is already attached; he will break your heart because nothing will deter his loyalty to his partner. The Page is very proud and will accept help from no one, though he will use his own boundless energy and strength to help others and fight for the disadvantaged.

Reverse Meanings

The Page of Wands reversed is warning you to beware of flattery from a false friend. This person is shallow and superficial and is only using you to achieve as much as he can as quickly as possible.

Knight of Wands

This card depicts a young man dressed in red and gold. He holds aloft a flaming torch while carrying a spear in the other hand. He journeys through the summer twilight over a hillside covered in ferns and heather.

The Symbolism

The Knight of Wands represents the mutable power of fire, volatile and changeable. The Knight of this card is on a quest, he stands on the threshold of an adventure and strides out boldly over the hillside at twilight. The torch he holds represents the power of his own inner fire to light his way through the darkness.

For the Celts, the twilight was mysterious, a time between times, between day and night. All such thresholds were magical—the place between the land and the sea, doorways, the time between one day and the next, the witching hour of midnight, the times between seasons. At such times, access to the Otherworld was possible between the thinning veils.

The foreground of the card shows the magical fern plant. Fern is a threshold plant, coming into its power at the turning of one season to another. It was a sacred plant of midsummer, which is the only safe time to gather its seed, when it is said to blossom like fire or gold, and can inspire prophetic dreams. On midsummer night, it ripens between midnight and one o'clock, then falls to the ground, disappearing instantly. In earlier times, people would make a charm for protection from the fern, which would be cut down to five fronds and smoked and hardened in the midsummer fire so that it looked like a gnarled hand.

Divinatory Meanings

The Knight of Wands represents the volatile and changeable nature of the element of fire. He calls on you to invoke the fire within. Where is your sense of adventure? Perhaps you lost it somewhere along the way? It is time to find it again. The world is full of new experiences, places to see and people to meet. Now you need to stretch and challenge yourself; you are on the threshold of exciting times. The Knight heralds a time of action, perhaps a sudden journey or a change of residence.

As with the other court cards, the Knight of Wands can represent a real person who influences a change in your life. He is an extrovert, brimming with restless energy. He loves a challenge and is virtually fearless, thriving on the stimulation of danger and risk. The Knight is intelligent, witty, charming, and humorous. His ideals are very high, he is a philosopher and a seeker after truth, he is incapable of lying. He hates any kind of unfairness or oppression and is often something of a rebel. The Knight is a warm, generous, loveable character who makes a wise and loyal friend, though his temper is quick to flare up if he thinks anyone is abusing his generosity. His temper is quite short-lived, however, and you would have to do something pretty bad or unjust to make an enemy of him, but if you do he is formidable. Be warned that the Knight of Wands is a free spirit and hates to be tied down. Romantically, he is a difficult proposition. Responsibility is not a word he likes. He needs the constant stimulation of new experiences, new horizons, and new ideas—settling down does not appeal to him.

Reverse Meanings

The Knight of Wands reversed is warning you to beware of a narrow-minded, bigoted person who loves to provoke arguments for their own sake. This person is unhappy because they don't have the courage to expand their lives and go after the things they want, and they envy those who do. You will find that they try to belittle your achievements and those of others. Remember, it's their problem, not yours.

Queen of Wands

The card depicts a handsome, red-haired woman clad in a flame-colored dress. About her forehead, she wears a chaplet of marigold flowers and clasps a spear in her right hand. She is accompanied by her fox familiar, and together they await the midsummer dawn before the needfire.

The Symbolism

The Queen of Wands represents the stable dimension of the element of fire. Hers is the hearth fire that lies at the heart of the home, warming, welcoming, and nurturing. With her spear she is prepared to defend her domain with the ferocity of a vixen defending her cubs.

In this illustration, she has lit the midsummer needfire from her own hearth flame. In the past, all the people would gather at the solstice eve on the nearest hilltop and light the bonfires of oak to encourage the sun to rise on the longest day at the zenith of its powers. The chain of fires and beacons could be seen blazing through the night across the country.

The Queen's animal familiar is the fox, an ancient inhabitant of Britain, cunning, wily, and clever enough to adapt to any environment, whether woodland, moorland, mountain, or even city. Very old foxes are said to have magical pearls of wisdom in their heads. The fox's red coat and its swiftness make it an emblem of fire and the sun. However, it is also a burrowing animal and a familiar guide to the Underworld, associated with the journey of the sun through the netherworld and its emergence at the winter solstice. The Northern Lights, the Aurora Borealis, are known as "the light of the fox."

Divinatory Meanings

The fire of the Queen of Wands nourishes and sustains as it inspires. Hers is the illumination of faith and vision that comes from within and that cannot be dimmed or extinguished by external sources. But just as the hearth fire needs to be fed, so does the flame of the spirit. This card calls on you to sustain your vision and nurture your spirit. It is time to develop the qualities of independence, creativity, and warmth.

The influence of the Queen of Wands may make itself felt in your life in the form of an actual woman. She is friendly and warm, but forthright and even a bit bossy. With the Queen, what you see is what you get. She is completely open and straightforward and detests people who employ subtleties and tricks to get what they want. Women who flutter their eyelashes and pretend helplessness earn her contempt. The Queen of Wands will tackle anything. Her home is always warm and welcoming and she rules it with a tireless energy and practical skill. Those whom she takes to her heart will find her a loyal and loving friend who provides both a strong shoulder to cry on and practical help in a crisis. Her strength does not derive from the perceptions or needs of others; she is completely independent, her will is strong, she is sure of who and what she is and arranges her world with a sure touch. She can be passionate, impulsive, and quick-tempered, though her rages never last long and she is incapable of holding a grudge. The Queen of Wands may be a successful career woman, as she is imaginative and creative, or she may focus her many talents on her home and children.

Reverse Meanings

The Queen of Wands reversed indicates that you will come into contact with a jealous woman. Her basic insecurity makes her imagine wrongs and she is quick to accuse others. She is domineering and likes to keep tight control on those in her sphere of influence by any means possible. She is mistress of the art of emotional blackmail and no amount of rational argument will dissuade her from her position.

Does this sound like someone you know? Unfortunately, there is no pleasing someone like this; whatever you do will never be enough. If she is a relative, treat her gently because she is an unhappy woman, but don't let her make you feel guilty, it really isn't your fault. You must live your life and follow your own dreams—she is unhappy precisely because she hasn't done this. Don't fall into the same trap.

Maybe, just maybe, this card is warning you that you are in danger of doing exactly this and becoming like the Queen of Wands reversed.

King of Wands

The card shows the Lord of the Powers of Fire depicted as a regal middle-aged man, with auburn hair and gray eyes, robed in crimson and crowned with golden oak leaves. In his hand, he holds a reed scepter bound with gold and tipped with the symbol of a flaming sun. He is seated on a golden throne that has armrests shaped as bull's heads; a wren perches on one of them. He inhabits a summer landscape. St. John's wort, yarrow, and camomile flowers grow at his feet. The background shows the midsummer sun standing high over Stonehenge.

The Symbolism

In this card, the King of Wands represents the Lord of the Powers of Fire. Magically, the element of fire is concerned with creativity, life energy, the spirit, and the strength of the will. It is associated with the direction of the south, the magical tool of the wand, inner sight, vision, and the festival of Coamhain, the summer solstice. Fire takes on many forms, from the gentle flicker of the candle flame to the warmth of the hearth fire, the light of the beacon, and the burning incandescence of the sun. It is the illumination of the spirit within.

At the midsummer solstice the Oak King, ruler of the light half of the year, is at the zenith of his powers. After this day, his spirit is taken to Caer Arianrhod, the whirling Spiral Castle, located in the Corona Borealis, which at midsummer is sinking over the horizon. Rulership of the waning year is passed to his brother the Holly King until the winter solstice, when he will take up the scepter once again.

In Britain there are oaks that have lived for thousands of years. The oak is an important totem of midsummer, where it stands at the turning of the season, looking back to the waxing year and forward to the waning year.

The Oak King's familiar bird is the wren. Wren ceremonies were enacted up to the nineteenth century and may well have dated from the Megalithic age. These ceremonies were conducted around the midwinter solstice, when rituals were performed to chase away the powers of darkness and the Oak King takes up his rulership of the year. The wren represented the death and rebirth of the sun at the winter solstice. In ogham, its name is *druen*,

related to *dur* or *oak*. It was hunted on St. Stephen's day and carried in procession by the wren boys. In Somerset, the wren was
carried about as "the King" in a glass box, surmounted by a wheel
on which there were various colored ribbons. He was symbolically
so big he had to be carried on a cart pulled by six horses, which
may represent the six months of his rule.

The wren is often paired with the robin, the familiar of the
Holly King, sometimes seen as the female to the robin's male.
They are sometimes thought to battle for rulership of the year.

The oak's familiar animal is the bull. In Britain, many old oaks
are known as "bull oaks," including Herne's oak in Windsor Forest.
The bull is also connected with thunder gods; its bellow sounds
like thunder. The strength and virility of the bull is the animal
kingdom's equivalent of the oak. When the mistletoe, semen of
the Forest Lord, was gathered from the sacred oak at midwinter,
two white bulls were chosen for sacrifice. When the ancients sacrificed the powerful and fertile bull, its blood was believed to
impart these qualities to the land. The bull is an ancient symbol of
power, fertility, and strength associated with kingship, the land,
and the sun.

In Celtic myth, the solar cart was pulled by three oxen, rather
than horses. For the Druids, the bull was the sun and the cow the
earth. The bull symbolizes the masculine, solar, generative forces
of the sky gods and the human king as representative of divine
power. It was ridden by solar heroes and gods, storm and sky gods
who brought the fertilizing power of the sun, rain, and thunder.

In Celtic countries, a druid would choose the High King by
undertaking the ceremony of *Tarbhfhess* or Bull Feast. A white bull
was sacrificed and the druid would eat his fill of the flesh of the
bull, drink its blood and broth, and sleep on its flayed hide while a
spell of truth was chanted over him, a vision quest to dream of the
rightful king.

Divinatory Meanings

In this card we meet the quintessential powers of fire in the guise of the King of Wands. Fire is regarded as the most spiritual of all the elements, with the flame as the material manifestation on the earthly plane of the element itself.

This card calls on you to develop the fiery part of your nature, the part linked to altruism, idealism, warmth of being, impulsiveness, and originality. Most of all, the King of Wands calls on you to learn the lesson of the bull. Bull is a mighty creature of mature masculine vigor and potency. Bull is often the familiar of a leader or high priest; its lesson is one of leadership and the determination and reliability that a leader needs. A leader will sacrifice many of his own needs for the good of his followers. A leader needs to be strong enough to carry his decisions through.

The influence of the King of Wands may be felt through an actual person in your life. He is a mature man who is a larger than life character, dynamic, lively, energetic, and a born leader. He has noble ideals and believes that human beings can, and should, be more than they are. When individuals fall short of his expectations, he is intolerant of their failure. Good causes and ideals are more important to him than material concerns or even personal relationships.

Reverse Meanings

If the King of Wands appears reversed in your spread, it indicates that you have too much fire in your nature, which causes you to be impulsive, irritable, autocratic, and completely intolerant of the attitudes of other people.

Here the King's familiar, the bull, may be telling you that you need patience and hard work to deal with your present situation. Are you being unjustly stubborn or prejudiced about something or someone? You could be acting with unreasonable jealousy or just plain vindictive. Obsession is unhealthy—take a logical, honest look at your situation.

Suit of Cups

Element: water

Season: autumn
Lughnasa day to Samhain Eve

Color: blue

Attributes: the emotions, intuition,
psychic abilities

Direction: west

Festival: Herfest, the autumn equinox

Ace of Cups

The card shows a golden cup inscribed with images from the Gunderstrup cauldron. It stands against a field of ripe corn ready for harvesting and is overhung with a bough of rosehips. A rainbow appears in the bright blue sky.

The Symbolism

The Ace of Cups is the root of the powers of water. It is the magical tool of the west brought from the mystical city of Murias. It appears in the various guises as grail, cauldron, and hollow of water.

The suit of cups corresponds to the element of water and the season of autumn. Its station on the wheel is Herfest, the autumn equinox, which marks the harvest and the completion of the vegetation cycle of the year as the days begin to grow colder and the light declines. It is the time of fullness and maturity.

Magically, water rules emotions and feelings, including love and hate, daring and cowardice, happiness and sorrow, giving and taking. It also rules the intuition and psychic skills. Water is cleansing and purifying. It is the power of experience.

Water can be the safety of the uterine waters of the womb, the cleansing stream, the deep pool of the subconscious mind, the nourishing river, the brew of initiation, the movement of the tides, and the power of the sea to give bounty or destroy with its tempest.

The cup in the picture can be interpreted as the Holy Grail, the cup of enlightenment; drinking from it brings about union with the Divine. In Christian lore, it takes the form of the chalice used at the Last Supper, which according to legend was brought to Britain by Joseph of Arimathea.

In legend, the knights of King Arthur search for the mysterious Grail, which will heal the sacred king of his wound and make whole the land, and facilitate the union of its finder with God. Various stories trace the adventures of the seekers. The quest of each knight is personal and individual, they undergo many tests and challenges to prove themselves worthy, loyal, and pure in heart; most fall by the wayside. The Holy Chalice is eventually found by Galahad, the Perfect Knight. Alone he has to face the powers and answer the question "Who does the grail serve?" He correctly answers, "It serves all."

The story of the Holy Grail has its origins in the earlier Celtic legends of magical cauldrons containing brews that can confer enlightenment, initiation, and rebirth, such as in the following legend.

The goddess Ceridwen lived on an island in the middle of a lake with her children, Creirwy ("Dear One"), the most beautiful girl in the world, and Afagddu ("Utter Darkness"), the ugliest boy. Ceridwen decided to help Afagddu overcome his disadvantages by brewing a potion for him that would contain all the wisdom of the Three Realms. The herbs were ritually collected and the cauldron brewed for a year and a day, stirred by a blind man and warmed by the breath of nine muses. A little boy, Gwion, was given the job of feeding the fire beneath it. One day, three drops fell from the cauldron onto his finger, which he put into his mouth to ease the pain. Instantly he was at one with all things past, present, and future. Furious that he had stolen the magic, Ceridwen pursued him in the form of a black hag. Gwion, using his new powers, changed himself into a hare but Ceridwen turned into a greyhound to catch him. Gwion jumped into a river and became a fish while Ceridwen proceeded to change herself into an otter and swam after him. He then flew from the river as a bird and Ceridwen became a hunting hawk. Hoping to elude her, Gwion transformed himself into a grain of wheat on the threshing floor of a granary, but the goddess, becoming a black hen, ate him. For nine months Gwion remained in the womb of the goddess, until at last he was reborn as a beautiful boy child.

The story of Gwion is a metaphor about initiation. First of all, he stokes the cauldron of knowledge, then, when he least expects it, he gains a new consciousness of All. The knowledge then makes him afraid and he tries to run away from it. The goddess challenges him by assuming a frightening form to test his worthiness. He goes through different personifications of animal totems, assimilating the knowledge of different realities, while the confrontation of the goddess forces him on, refining his being. Eventually he has to be reassumed into the womb of the goddess in order to be reborn as a true initiate.

Magically, the rose symbolizes mystical or divine love, here depicted as ripe rosehips hanging over the cup. Traditionally, the hip represents the womb of the Mother Goddess and demonstrates her bounty at the harvest, when the promise of the year comes to fruition and the cycle is completed.

The rainbow represents hope and the eternal spirit, and was seen as the pathway to the afterlife. It symbolizes connection to the enduring spirit, or Higher Self, and the continuance of the Self throughout incarnations.

Divinatory Meanings

The Ace of Cups is the root of the powers of water. Water is liquid, like the blood that flows through your veins. All life started in the rich biological soup of the oceans, just as you were protected by the uterine waters of your mother's womb. It is the element associated with emotions, feelings, instincts, and the subconscious mind.

The cup is placed at the station of the west, which on the Wheel is the time of the autumn equinox when the harvest is completed.

All of the aces indicate a burst of raw energy. With the Ace of Cups this relates to an overwhelming rush of feelings and emotions. When the Ace of Cups appears in your spread, it indicates a time of great spiritual fulfillment and contact with the Source of Being. Your soul feels its connection with the cosmos and is nourished by Divine love. You are aware of free flowing energies and your spirit is healed and bathed in joy. It may be that you receive spiritual healing or become aware of your own healing powers. You may receive guidance from the Higher Self or contact guides and spirits.

The Ace of Cups also heralds creative inspiration and the production of works of beauty. You may discover a new talent.

This card is also strongly associated with the home and with the love and contentment to be found there. It portends a happy relationship, perhaps marriage and parenthood. Your home will be a welcoming place. Interesting and pleasant visitors are indicated, as well as parties and celebrations.

Reverse Meanings

When the Ace of Cups appears reversed, it points to feelings of unhappiness and isolation. Perhaps, because of some hurt, you have tried to block out feelings altogether. You feel that you have lost your way and you doubt things that you were once sure about—your direction in life and your spiritual beliefs. At some point in life, everyone goes through this "dark night of the soul"; it shakes loose illusions, tests and tempers you, and ultimately makes you stronger.

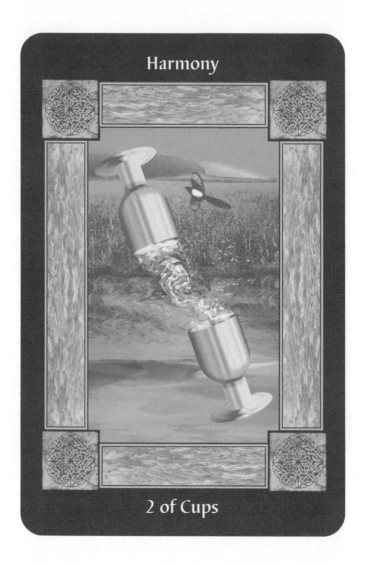

Two of Cups

The card depicts two identical golden cups pouring sparkling water from one to the other. The background shows a sunlit stream in front of a field in the early autumn. Daisies and poppies grow on the bank and a magpie appears to the right of the cups.

The Symbolism

Here the raw energy of the Ace of Cups becomes polarized. The two cups depicted are equally balanced and maintain an equilibrium by pouring the water they contain back and forth. Water in a tarot card always represents the emotions and the subconscious mind. Here the water is clear and free-flowing.

The magpie is also symbolic of balance. It has contrasting black and white plumage. In northern England, the magpie was thought to be a hybrid of the raven and the dove and so could not be classified as either a herald of the Underworld or the heavens, but has both realms balanced within it. It is therefore considered to have especially mysterious properties. There are several well-known children's rhymes concerning the portent of the appearance of particular numbers of magpies; this is a folk memory of the times when they were important birds of augury. The magpie was known as a witch familiar and associated with magic, a familiar of the divine trickster.

Divinatory Meanings

The raw emotional energy of the Ace of Cups now begins to make itself manifest in the world in the Two of Cups as one person interacts with another. This card calls on you to recognize that there is harmony in polarity—male and female, night and day, summer and winter—and that that these opposites are necessary to existence and have equal value.

When the Two of Cups appears in your spread, it heralds a phase of harmony and cooperation in the area of relationships. Quarrels and differences in existing relationships are resolved and you may begin new friendships or even a new romance. Success will come from working with other people; you will be able to bounce ideas off each other and come up with something new. According to surrounding cards, the Two of Swords may indicate contractual and business arrangements.

Reverse Meanings

The Two of Cups reversed indicates that quarrels and misunder-standings mar relationships—even separation and divorce are pos-sible. According to surrounding cards it can be warning you that a partner is being unfaithful, or that your love is not returned in equal measure.

Magpie may be telling you that you are off balance. Are you only seeing what you want to see in a situation or a person, ignor-ing a possible darker side? Magpie likes to collect bright and sparkly things, but all that glitters is not gold. Don't be fooled by a superficial glamour. Magpie teaches the way of augury, of reading omens and signs. Magpie reminds us of the need for balance—you may need to balance the practical side of yourself with the dreamer in order to manifest the dream in the world. You may need to recognize that there must be endings as well as beginnings, light as well as dark. The growth of the year at Beltane initiates the death of the year at Samhain.

Three of Cups

This card shows three handsome cups decorated with growing cornflowers and greenery.

The Symbolism

The harvest is the completion and resolution of the farming year. It began at Lughnasa with the gathering of the first fruits, and carried on until around the autumn equinox and Harvest Home.

From the earliest times, the farmer recognized that he worked within the powerful cycle of the seasons, and the pattern of the year must be observed. There was a time to plant, a time to weed the growing crops, and finally, a time to harvest and collect new seeds before the whole cycle began again. Our ancestors sought the help of the gods to ensure favorable weather—enough water to nourish, enough sun to ripen, holding back the winter frosts until the harvest had been gathered. Rituals and observances were taken to ensure such help, as without them it was not even certain that the spring would return after the winter, or that the sun would be reborn and gain strength after the winter solstice.

The soil itself was part of the Mother Goddess, her body, and was treated with respect and venerated as the giver of fertility. If any drink were taken into the fields, a small amount would be poured as a libation to the earth—a very different attitude from today's when pesticides and chemical fertilizers destroy the natural balance to squeeze more crops from ground impoverished by lack of proper management. An old proverb stated that a farmer should live as though he were going to die tomorrow, but farm as though he were going to live forever.

The culmination of the year, and the reward for all the hard work, was the harvest. It was a time for celebration, and farms competed with each other to see who would finish first. The last load was taken home with great rejoicing and was followed by the harvest supper, which involved much feasting and drinking, singing, and making speeches. The place of honor at the feast would be given to the corn dolly, fashioned from the last sheaf to be cut, in which the Corn Spirit was thought to have retreated. The dolly would be kept until the following Plough Monday, when it was ploughed under the fields to return the spirit to the earth.

Divinatory Meanings

The threes represent an initial completion of the first stage of a project or life cycle, and though this can be celebrated, there is more to come, just as the completion of the harvest marks the end of one cycle and the start of another.

When the Three of Cups appears in your spread, it indicates that affairs come to a happy conclusion. According to surrounding cards, this may be the success of a project, the start of a love affair, a marriage, the birth of a child, or recovery from an illness. It is time for celebrations, and you will entertain family and friends and be given hospitality in return. You will feel vital and alive. This is a time of great emotional and spiritual growth. All differences and quarrels will be resolved and relationships will be loving and trusting.

Spiritually, this is time to give thanks for blessings received. Remember—*thank you* are words of power.

Reverse Meanings

The Three of Cups reversed indicates that you have been excessively and destructively self-indulgent, whether eating too much, smoking too much, drinking too much, taking drugs, or engaging in selfishly promiscuous sex with no thought for the feelings of others. This behavior is making you ill and stems from a poor self-image. You need to look at why you are doing this to yourself and deal with the underlying problem.

Four of Cups

This card shows four rusting cups standing in front of a dripping yew tree in a hazy landscape.

The Symbolism

The four cups depicted in the card are neglected, they have become rusty and dull. They stand in front of a yew, a tree with sinister connotations. The yew is generally seen as a tree of death, though this is only part of its lore. Yew berries are deadly poisonous and their toxin was used to poison arrowheads, daggers, and spears.

The yew, however, is also a tree of regeneration arising from death. As the central trunk becomes old, the insides decay—but a new tree grows within the spongy dying mass of the old. In Brittany, it is said that a churchyard yew will send a root to the mouth of each corpse. This root is a symbol of the spirit reborn in much the same way as the tree is reborn. The yew reminds us that out of any kind of death or ending, a new life begins.

Divinatory Meanings

All of the fours indicate some kind of discontent. This card demonstrates that you are feeling discontent on an emotional level.

The Four of Cups indicates that difficulties within a relationship have led to unspoken resentments and a lack of emotional fulfillment. You might be tempted to have an affair but this is not the answer. You need to look realistically at the relationship—you may have based it on false assumptions, thinking it should fulfill your fantasy of what a relationship should be, rather than trying to build a real understanding between two real individuals.

You are bored and dissatisfied with your life, you feel apathetic and uninspired. You may be tempted to relieve this with excessive indulgence in materialistic pleasures, but this will soon pall and will not fill the gap you feel. You need to re-examine your lifestyle—what it is that you want and how you can achieve it. Your way of life does not provide you with goals to reach for; you are not stretched or sufficiently stimulated.

Reverse Meanings

The Four of Cups reversed indicates that you have been trying to gain transitory satisfactions in life from seeking ever greater novelties and excitements, but in reality these have brought you little pleasure. You quickly grow bored and sated with each new thing and continue to search for what will really satisfy you. This card is telling you that contentment can only come from within, from being happy with yourself. You need to achieve something you can be proud of, not merely be entertained.

Five of Cups

This card shows two cups wrapped with bindweed. They have fallen over and their contents have spilled. Three cups remain standing and are full of liquid. In the background is Dozemary Pool in Cornwall, illuminated by the moon.

The Symbolism

Bindweed strangles anything that it climbs around and is a symbol of dangerous obstinacy. It is said that the climbing bindweed twines from left to right and cannot be persuaded to do otherwise. In the card, it has toppled two cups and spilled their contents, while three other cups, still full, remain ignored.

The background of the card is Dozemary Pool. It lies isolated, high on Bodmin Moor—a lonely place, brooding and mysterious. The vicinity is said to be haunted by a dark spirit, sad and tormented. This may be a folk memory of some Celtic god, but the Cornish identify it with the spirit of Jan Tregeagle, doomed to eternal torment for his sins in life. Tregeagle was a real person, a stern magistrate in the early 1600s who was corrupt and unpopular. According to legend, he sold his soul to the devil. His spirit was condemned to attempt the impossible task of emptying the bottomless lake of Dozemary with a perforated limpet shell.

Dozemary Pool also has another legend associated with it: it is one of the several sites said to have been the body of water where Sir Bedevere returned Arthur's sword to the Lady of the Lake.

After the last great battle, King Arthur lay mortally wounded, tended only by one remaining knight, Sir Bedevere. Knowing that his magic sword, Excalibur, must be returned from whence it came, he drew it from its scabbard and asked Bedevere to take it to a nearby body of water and throw it in. Bedevere set off, but thinking it a pity to discard such a fine sword, hid it and returned to the king. Arthur asked him what he saw as the sword entered the water. Bedevere replied "only the wind on the waves" and Arthur knew that he had not done as he asked. Once again he asked the knight to fulfill his request. Again Bedevere failed to throw in the sword, thinking the future of Albion might lie with it. Hiding it in some rushes he returned to Arthur who asked him what he saw. "Only the wind on the waves," said Bedevere. Arthur chided the knight for failing to carry out his king's last request, and ashamed, Bedevere returned to the lake and threw in Excalibur. The sword described a shining arc, and as it fell toward the lake, a woman's arm, clad in white samite, rose from the lake. The beautiful hand clasped the sword and held it high before descending with it into the depths of the water. When Bedevere told Arthur what he had seen, the king knew that this time his faithful knight had carried out his request and that Excalibur was safe in the keeping of the Lady of the Lake until Albion should need it again.

Divinatory Meanings

When the Five of Cups appears in your spread, it indicates that you are wallowing in regret for something you have lost and ignoring what you still have left, which may be more valuable in the long run. This card often indicates a marriage or a love affair gone wrong, leading to unhappiness and perhaps separations, but in this card the situation is not terminal, there is something that can be retrieved. You seem to be trying to avoid making decisions, hoping that by ignoring a situation it will go away.

Reverse Meanings

The Five of Cups reversed indicates an unexpected and rapid change, overturning your whole way of life. This is the source of much anxiety. However, this change is paving the way for a new kind of life, with different expectations and new friendships.

Six of Cups

The six cups of this card appear faintly against a stand of cypress trees. In the background is Glendalough in Ireland.

The Symbolism

The six cups are ephemeral since they belong to the past—they are a memory. They appear against a background of cypress trees—a tree of mourning and a reminder of the inevitability of deaths and endings of all kinds. As such, it was used at funerals and memorial services to remember and honor the dead. However, it is an evergreen tree and reminds us of the incorruptible nature of the spirit. In our tradition, cypress needles are used as the incense at the dead time of winter, and at the seasonal death of the Corn Spirit at Herfest, where it mourns his passing and reminds us that life continues and will be renewed. At Yule it is an evergreen decoration and shows us that the life spirit remains, even in the dark time.

Divinatory Meanings

You are trying to escape into the past, which you are remembering as happy and beautiful. You can recall past events and enjoy the memory, but you must recognize that these things have irrevocably vanished and cannot be recaptured in reality. Instead of wallowing in nostalgia, use the knowledge you have gained from the past to realize your ambitions in the present.

Depending on the surrounding cards, the Six of Cups can mean that an old friend or lover comes back into your life, and though you cannot regain what you had before, you can begin a totally new and different kind of relationship.

Spiritually, this card is telling you that you will gain insight by exploring the ancient traditions of your own people, rather than trying to adopt those of foreign cultures.

Reverse Meanings

When the Six of Cups appears reversed in your spread, it indicates that you absolutely refuse to let go of the past. You try to cling to old customs and habits when they no longer have any meaning or benefit. It may be that the memory of your past glories and successes is preventing you from achieving anything now, for fear of not matching up.

Seven of Cups

The card shows seven cups—or does it? The background is the
Rollright Stones in Oxfordshire, England.

The Symbolism

The seven cups of this card distort and dissolve and may be illusory. Perhaps you only think you see them. They are shown against a background of hops, which are used to make beer.

The Rollright Stones, also in the background, consist of a stone circle called The King's Men, a standing stone called the King Stone, and a burial chamber called the Whispering Knights. They are a Bronze Age temple on the border of Oxfordshire and Warwickshire, about 100 feet in diameter. It is said that no one has ever been able to count the stones, and that anyone who does, and gets the same number twice, will die. Actually, there are seventy-two.

According to legend, they are a king and his army turned into stone by a witch. The army had conquered all England as far as the village of Little Rollright and the king marched up the hill only to be met by a witch who announced to him, "Seven long strides thou shall take! If Long Compton thou canst see, King of England thou shalt be!" Long Compton is just over the brow of the hill, so confidently the king took seven great strides forward, but his view was blocked by a mound. Laughing, the witch turned the king and his men into stones and herself into an elder tree. As the tree bloomed at midsummer, the blossom would be cut by the local populace, and it is said that the king turned his head to watch. Fairies are said to live in the mound upon which the King Stone stands and to come out at night to dance around it. The stones are also said to come alive at midnight, or at least at New Year, when they perform strange dances and go down to the nearby brook for a drink.

Divinatory Meanings

You are deceiving yourself. You might think you are achieving something, but you are deluded. Not only are you lying to yourself, but you are treating your friends badly, breaking promises, and being unreliable. You might have committed yourself to too many things to achieve any of them. You need to look at your situation more realistically. A lot of opportunities surround you, but you cannot keep all the options open forever. Surrounding cards will indicate whether these choices relate to several suitors, or business, creative, or social opportunities. You must make a decision based on careful consideration to make any of the possibilities a reality.

Spiritually, you might think you have had a mystical experience, but you are confusing fact with fantasy and wishful thinking. Do not follow the path of illusion, it is a dead end. Illumination cannot be obtained by shortcuts or drugs; it cannot be bought.

Reverse Meanings

The Seven of Cups reversed indicates that you have been relying on the false promises of others. Do not be carried away by the over-enthusiasm of so-called friends; you might be drawn into a situation that is difficult to escape. Depending on surrounding cards, this can relate to alcohol or drug addiction. You are letting real opportunities pass you by and would rather escape into a fantasy life. What is it that you are afraid of in the real world? Why do you want to hide from it?

Eight of Cups

The card shows eight discarded cups. They lie abandoned and entwined with ivy and cinquefoil flowers. The background is a mountainous region in Killarney, Ireland, in autumn.

The Symbolism

Mountains symbolize the aspirations of the spirit. Mystics, poets, and seekers after truth would often seek a period of isolation in the mountains, leaving behind their everyday life and the company of their fellow men to journey in a realm closer to the gods.

The ivy that binds the cups has the power to change consciousness, to facilitate an inward journey. Along with the vine, bramble, fig, plane tree, briar rose, primrose, periwinkle, cinquefoil, and some poplars, the ivy has five-pointed leaves and is therefore sacred to the Goddess. The ivy represents her throughout the Wheel of the Year and the cycle of death and rebirth. It represents the spiral dance of life with its spiral growth and the spiral arrangement of leaves. The spiral is a double one: inward toward the Self then outward to share and use the knowledge among the others we meet in the dance.

During the Middle Ages, cinquefoil had the reputation of being a magical herb. It was widely associated with witches and believed to have been used in the "flying ointment," which facilitated journeys to other realms, though it has no narcotic properties.

Divinatory Meanings

The Eight of Cups talks about the necessity of letting something go. Sometimes it is necessary to recognize that a bad situation cannot be changed or resolved and must simply be abandoned and left behind. This may involve a change of residence or a period of travel. Often the ending of such a situation is accompanied by depression and regret, but this letting go is the beginning of a change that is necessary to bring something new and fresh into your life, a turning point in your life that will bring you new friends and experiences.

Spiritually, you may be called upon to leave behind material success for something higher. The ivy of the card represents the change of consciousness that takes place at initiation, bringing with it the gifts of prophecy and vision. It teaches the lesson of sacrifice: the old self must be left behind or "die" before a spiritual rebirth can take place.

Reverse Meanings

The Eight of Cups reversed indicates the reckless abandonment of a carefully constructed and well-founded way of life in a misguided search for an ideal, whether this is a person or a concept. It may be that you are looking to someone else to supply what you lack within yourself. This is not possible, you can recognize that some people have qualities and outlooks that you don't, but these cannot be possessed through another, they have to be developed within yourself.

Nine of Cups

The card shows nine rich, polished cups decorated with poppy flowers and clover. The background is Glastonbury Tor.

The Symbolism

The nine cups of this card are well looked after and reflect the prosperity and stable circumstances of their owner. They are surrounded by poppy flowers, sometimes said to be the "mother of the corn," and clover leaves. Clover has always been highly regarded and associated with the Triple Goddess, the Celtic sunwheel, and later the Christian trinity. The four-leafed clover represents the four directions and the four elements. Clover is associated with Otherworldly sight as a visionary herb and with all four elements and is used to balance the Self and to consecrate copper tools.

The tower on the summit of Glastonbury Tor is dedicated to St. Michael, an earlier church having been destroyed by an earthquake. According to Arthurian legend, it was the fortress of King Melwas, ruler of the Summerland, the kingdom of the Isle of Apples or Avalon, both a real place of apple orchards in the South of England, and the mystical realm to which the soul travels at death or initiation.

Divinatory Meanings

The Nine of Cups is sometimes called "the Wish Card" and heralds the fulfillment of a dream. It shows that difficulties have been overcome and that all your efforts and steady commitment will be rewarded. This is a time of emotional and material stability, good health, and great happiness, though this situation may only be temporary.

Spiritually, this card is telling you that you must take time to assimilate what you have learned and must work on balancing the elements within yourself to create a firm foundation of knowledge and strength before you try to progress further.

Reverse Meanings

The Nine of Cups appearing reversed in your spread indicates that you are guilty of great irresponsibility. You are being very selfish and self-indulgent, using your friends and abusing their hospitality.

You are spending money that you don't have, and this will lead to financial difficulties, if it hasn't already. This situation cannot go on for much longer, even though your vanity and complacency tells you it can. People will soon have had enough of your behavior and will no longer have anything to do with you. Relationships are founded on give and take. If you want real friendships and real love, you must learn to give as well as take.

Reward

10 of Cups

Ten of Cups

This card depicts ten beautiful cups brimming over with the fruits of the harvest—apples, corn, hazelnuts, and acorns.

The Symbolism

The ten cups of this card are filled with the various good things of the harvest, the culmination of all the efforts of the farming year. They represent achievements of various kinds. The fruits depicted all have various symbolic meanings and energies, and play their part in our harvest celebrations.

The apple harvest begins at Lughnasa, which falls at the beginning of August in high summer. It is a time of warmth, strength, and fruitfulness, when the Corn Lord is honored with Lammas Wool (from the Gaelic *La Mas Nbhal* or "feast of the apple gathering"), a hot spiced drink of cider and ale with toast or pieces of apple floating in it. Each person takes out a piece and wishes good luck to everyone present before eating it and passing the cup on.

The acorn appears as the representative of the Oak King, the ruler of the light half of the year who surrendered his rulership at the midsummer solstice to the Holly King. The seed acorn is the promise of his return at the midwinter solstice when the sun will be reborn and the days grow longer.

The hazel is the primary power tree of the autumn equinox. In ogham the hazel is *coll*, one of the seven chieftain trees. The sacredness of the hazel to the Celts is demonstrated by the death penalty that was carried out on anyone foolish enough to fell a hazel tree. The hazel fruits after nine years and in the ninth month of the year.

The bramble or blackberry was a sacred plant of the Celts. In Scotland, along with the rowan and the yew, it constituted the sacred fire. In ogham it is *muin* and honored as a tree, even though it is merely a bush. The five-petalled flowers associate the blackberry very strongly with the Goddess, and the fruit, which appears green at first, then red, and finally black, represents the three stages of the Goddess and the completion of the cycle.

Divinatory Meanings

The Ten of Cups indicates that you are now reaping the rewards of all your efforts. It is a time of great happiness within the family and you will experience the joy of true friendships. Your achievements are recognized and admired. This situation has firm foundations and will be long lasting. According to surrounding cards, you may receive some good news that leads to success when you least expect it.

Reverse Meanings

The Ten of Cups reversed indicates that your well-ordered environment will be interrupted in an extreme fashion, perhaps by the birth of a child or a troublesome teenager. This card heralds family quarrels and the loss of friendships.

Page of Cups

The card shows a young man with brown hair and blue eyes. His expression is thoughtful and reflective. He wears a blue costume and holds a silver cup. He kneels before a well surrounded by hazel trees, which drop nuts into the water. A salmon surfaces from the pond to consume the nuts.

The Symbolism

In Celtic legend, nine hazel trees of poetry overhung Connla's well. All the knowledge of the arts and sciences were given to these nine trees. The nuts dropped into the well and were eaten by the salmon that swam there, who developed one bright spot on his body for every nut he ate. These trees produced beauty (flowers) and wisdom (fruit) at the same time, and eating the nuts from these trees conferred all knowledge and wisdom to the one that ate them. Nuts are a Celtic symbol of concentrated wisdom, the sweetness of knowledge contained.

The salmon was regarded as a store of ancient knowledge and wisdom by the Celts and was one of the five oldest animals. The spotted salmon, by virtue of having eaten the hazel nuts, both contained and were symbols of all knowledge. If a person were to catch and eat one of these salmon, the wisdom would be transferred to them.

Fintan was the Salmon of Knowledge in Irish lore. Originally, he was human and survived the great flood, hiding in a cave in salmon form for centuries, gaining wisdom and knowledge of all that went on in Ireland. The giant Finegas hunted the fish along the banks of the Boyne for seven years, eventually catching it and setting it to roast, watched by his pupil Fionn mac Cumhal. Fionn burned his finger on the hot flesh and placed it in his mouth, and thus acquired all the knowledge of the salmon. Afterward, he had only to place his thumb in his mouth to have foreknowledge of events.

As a familiar, Salmon teaches ancestral knowledge, the initiation of water and healing. Salmon teaches how to balance and use the emotions to develop the spirit. Salmon teaches about enduring the trials of initiation and that anything is possible if you are single-minded enough to pursue it.

Divinatory Meanings

The Page of Cups represents the first impulse of the element of water, the initial development of the capacities of feeling and intuition. The pool he gazes into represents the soul, reflecting back the image of the true self. Reflection is the opposite of action, and leads down into making contact with the muse or *anima*. This card may herald a time of great perception and awareness, a time of spiritual development and understanding. The Salmon of Wisdom may be telling you to make up your mind if have been irresolute. Indecision can mean that you are achieving nothing and getting frustrated and angry with yourself, and taking it out on others.

On a personal level, this card is telling you that a hurt in the past damaged your self-esteem and self-confidence. You have been through a period of withdrawal and self-preoccupation. You are now learning to value yourself again and beginning to feel capable of loving once more. It is only by recognizing your own value that true love with another can be established. If you are looking to another to supply what is lacking in yourself, rather than treating the other as a separate person, the relationship is doomed to failure. This card can herald a new relationship, or a new level in an existing relationship.

Spiritually, passive meditation will prove to be of the most benefit to you at the moment. You have been badly hurt and this has left its scars. You need to learn to be at peace with yourself. It is not the time to join a group or perform rituals.

A court card often indicates the entrance of a person into your life, or a friend or acquaintance who proves important. The Page of Cups is an intense young man or woman whose carefully controlled exterior masks the volcano of emotions that lie within. It is difficult to really know the Page; he does not let his feelings show and is very suspicious of other people's motives. He doesn't like to let anyone get too close. He never forgets a kindness or an injury and will reward or punish accordingly with a ruthless determination. The Page is a philosophical young person, interested in religion and the fundamental questions of life and death, but his views are his own, and influenced by no one. He does not care what others think of him, and if you ask for his opinion he will give it with brutal honesty, not caring if he hurts your feelings.

Reverse Meanings

If the Page of Cups appears reversed in your spread, it indicates the appearance of a selfish and bitter person in your life who reacts to small or imagined injuries with furious hatred and schemes of revenge. This person can harbor a grudge for years.

The Page reversed may be telling you that it is time to let go of grudges or feelings of bitterness before they poison you and make you deeply depressed or even physically ill.

Knight of Cups

This card shows the Knight of Cups. He is a young man with brown hair and gray eyes. His silvery-blue armor is made from fish scales. He stands in the current of a stream and is holding a silver cup aloft, while an otter surfaces in the water before him. In the background, the autumn landscape of bearing apple trees stretches away to the sea.

The Symbolism

The Knight of Cups represents the changeable nature of the element of water, which is like the stream he stands in, constantly moving and shifting. This chivalrous Knight is scouring the earth in search of his ideal of beauty and truth, the Holy Grail.

The otter, which surfaces before him, often appears in legend as a guide to those undertaking voyages or quests. In every Celtic tongue, the otter is called "water dog" and shares some symbolism of the dog. The otter was much prized for its magical skin. Fishermen used to hunt otters with a three-pronged spear, a symbol of the water god, for its waterproof pelt. The speed with which the otter catches the Salmon of Wisdom made it a natural choice for an otter-skin hunting suit used in sympathetic magic when hunting wisdom. The skin also made the traditional bag for the Celtic harp and was used as a lucky lining for shields.

Divinatory Meanings

When the Knight of Cups appears in your spread, he may be telling you that it is time to open yourself up to the feeling of being in love. A heady romantic relationship is on its way to you, and you may even receive a proposal of marriage, which will be indicated by surrounding cards. On the other hand, you may receive a proposal of an artistic or creative nature from a man, or an invitation or message. Opportunities should be seized; they will not present themselves again.

Spiritually, this card relates to the lessons of the otter. In Irish tradition, the otter was sacred to the sea god Manannan, Lord of Deep Magic, and the otter guards many profound magical secrets. The jewel it reputedly possesses in its head is the pearl of wisdom, and even the skin of the otter was a power object. The otter catches the Salmon of Knowledge, and its form was adopted by deities and magicians in order to partake of its learning.

Otter familiars teach the way to go beyond the surface of a particular teaching or tradition to reach the core of truth that lies within it. Otter is concerned with truth, not dogma. Otter is a creature of earth and water and teaches you how to balance these elements within yourself. You need to be practical to get things done, but you need to dream to know what is worth doing. A whole person knows how to work hard, but also how to play and enjoy the simple pleasures of life. Otter catches the Salmon of Wisdom by being fluid and swift, not serious and ponderous.

The Knight of Cups may mark the appearance in your life of a man. He is creative and artistic, charming and good natured, caring nothing for money or status. He is a romantic with high ideals and can always be counted on to champion the underdog—the very model of the chivalrous knight. He hates to be restricted and likes to be free to follow his dreams. He values beauty and truth above all else and searches for perfection. He often hopes to find it mirrored in a partner, and should she fail to match up, he moves on, constantly hopeful of finding his soul mate. Should the magic feeling of "being in love" fade into the mundane, he will leave. He is seeking the perfection of a love that has a spiritual dimension, and for him sex is a holy sacrament that should touch the spirit. Though the knight is gentle and kind, he can leave many broken hearts in his wake when human women fail to match his ideals.

Reverse Meanings

The Knight of Cups reversed is warning you about an untrustworthy man in your life. He is idle, selfish, and incapable of telling the truth. He is too lazy to actually achieve anything, he just dreams about it and talks about it, telling himself that he is preparing himself for when the opportunity arises. If you are not careful, he could obtain money from you on false pretenses.

Perhaps the above is describing you? Are you in danger of retreating from participating in life, escaping through drug or alcohol abuse or into dreams? If so, you may experience episodes of despondency and nightmares. Take a lesson from the otter who is a creature of both water and earth, supple and fluid but quick and purposeful. You need to bring more of the earth element into your life, get involved with practical projects that demand physical labor and contact with the earth.

Queen of Cups

The card shows a dreamy woman holding a silver cup as she rises from the center of a lake. A kingfisher flashes across the water and in the background is Glastonbury Tor, Somerset.

The Symbolism

The woman of this card is the Grail Maiden, who holds the sacred chalice of enlightenment. According to legend, the Holy Grail was hidden in the Chalice Well, which springs at the bottom of Chalice Hill at Glastonbury, by Joseph of Arimathea, who brought it from the Holy Land. It is said that the well contains the precious blood—the water is red and rich in iron—and it is credited with many healing miracles. However, Glastonbury was a holy place and the well a healing shrine at least 1,000 years before Christianity.

Glastonbury Tor is a conical hill that can be seen from miles around. Its ridges form a spiral path to the summit, and following them in the correct way is said to give access to the Otherworld—the fairy realm of Annwn, ruled by King Gwyn ap Nudd, the Lord of the Underworld, who is sometimes said to be the leader of the Wild Hunt. For the Celts, Glastonbury was the Ynys-witrin, the Isle of Glass, where the souls and bodies of the dead were separated and received by the Underworld King.

According to some, Glastonbury is the legendary Isle of Avalon since it once became an island each winter as the surrounding land flooded, before the swamps were drained. All islands were sacred to the Celts. Arthur is said to have been transported to Avalon in a magical barge at the point of his death, where he will sleep until Britain shall need him again. The name Avalon comes from the Welsh *afal,* which means *apple.* The apple symbolizes the sun and immortality. There are many legendary Isles of Apples, which always lie in the west, the place of the setting sun, where it will enter the Underworld and journey to its point of rebirth in the east. Every soul was promised the same journey, as exemplified by the story of the Sacred King.

The nearby abbey claimed that Arthur was buried within its precincts. A grave opened in the twelfth century was found to contain a tall man and a woman and an inscription that stated, "Here in the Isle of Avalon the famous King Arthur lies buried." It is said that the bones were scattered and lost at the time of the dissolution of the monasteries.

The kingfisher is an elusive bird, rarely seen except as a bright, brief flash of blue over the water. It represents a moment of magic, a brief but significant connection with the Otherworld.

Divinatory Meanings

The Queen of Cups represents the stable dimension of the element of water contained within the still pool, the deep well, the cup, the cauldron, or depths of the psyche.

She embodies the mystery of the feminine, exerting a seductive power that has nothing to do with physical beauty—in fact, the Grail Maiden was not beautiful, her beauty was an inner one, a perfect spirit. The feminine mystery is connected to the secret and subconscious power of feelings. The Queen of Cups is attractive because she reflects back to the observer one's own inner desires. Because she is unknowable, men find her all the more seductive, as she can reflect their own fantasies. She reminds women to stop thinking of themselves purely as mother, housekeeper, or career woman, and reaffirm the mysterious and sensuous side of their natures.

The appearance of the Queen of Cups heralds a time of discovering new qualities and depths within yourself, an active and healthy inner life. She is telling you to explore and experience your feelings and pay attention to your feminine side, whether you are a man or a woman. Water is the element of intuition and psychic skills; these are abilities you possess and should learn to trust.

The Queen of Cups can indicate the appearance of a woman in your life. She may appear rather languid and dreamy. She likes the attention of others but doesn't do anything overt to attract it. She is a fragile creature who is easily hurt, and once hurt, she will withdraw into the solitude of her home, which she loves as her retreat and castle. She is highly imaginative and artistic, intuitive, and possibly clairvoyant. She appears to have great mysterious depths to her psyche that are unfathomable to the observer. She is compassionate toward her fellow beings and can be very motherly. She will help you in a crisis, but will probably wait to see if anyone else will do it first.

Reverse Meanings

The Queen of Cups reversed is telling you that you are out of touch with your feelings. Perhaps you are trying to block them off to prevent being hurt. This is not a happy or healthy state of affairs and will cause you psychological damage in the long run. Everyone is hurt sometimes; this is part of the human condition and no one is immune. Learning to deal with it is part of the process of becoming a complete and balanced person. Conversely, perhaps you are overwhelmed by your emotions and making yourself ill with worry and anxiety.

If this does not apply, the Queen of Cups reversed may be warning you about an unreliable woman who cannot be trusted or depended on. Her opinions change swiftly and without logic or just reason. One minute she might seem to be your best friend and the next your worst enemy. She is emotionally unstable, overwhelmed by her feelings, and inclined to hysteria. She will probably try to involve you in her largely imagined problems, but sympathy and encouragement in this area are the last things she needs.

Water

King of Cups

King of Cups

The card shows the King of Cups, Lord of the Powers of Water, a middle-aged man in blue robes lounging idly on a silver throne. He wears a crown of silver and pearls and clasps a silver cup of new wine in his hand. At his feet stands his faithful companion, an

Irish wolfhound. He contemplates the ripeness of the autumn equinox in a lush landscape that stretches away to the sea.

The Symbolism

The King of Cups is Lord of the Powers of Water. Magically, water rules the emotions and feelings, intuition, and psychic abilities. It is associated with the season of autumn, fullness and maturity, twilight, and the direction of the west. Its station on the wheel is Herfest, the autumn equinox marking the maturity of the year and the completion of the vegetation cycle. After the equinox, the light declines, the days grow shorter, and the weather begins to chill toward winter.

Blackberries provide the Herfest wine, which the King is drinking, described as "the blood of the earth pressed smooth." The blackberry is sacred to the Sidhe, the fairy folk of the mounds, into whose care the slain Harvest Lord is given. He becomes the King of the Underworld until the time of his rebirth at Yule.

In this card, the King of Cups is depicted sitting on a throne overlooking the sea. All types of water are symbolically related from the oceans that surround the land, rivers, streams, lakes, pools, and the falling rain, to the life blood that flows through the body, the nourishing fluid of the uterine water of the womb, and the masculine life force of the semen. Water represents the life force in its fluid state; it is near the beginning and the source of life and is the oldest of the divine powers. It is the first principle from which form arises. It refers to the unconscious life and the soul, where feelings reside. Water is concerned with sensitivity, reflection, and fluidity—an impressionable principle that needs to be contained to be given form.

The King is accompanied by his dog, which acts as both a companion and a guard. As well as being a mundane guardian, it is also a guardian of the threshold, Underworld treasure, and the boundaries between the worlds. The dog was often seen as conveying the soul to the Otherworld. In some legends of the Underworld, the entrance is through water, and ghostly dogs lead travelers into

pools and drown the unprepared. This represents the perilous journey of the spirit into the Underworld of the subconscious mind
toward the true Self.

Divinatory Meanings

The King of Cups represents the quintessential powers of water.
He is calling on you to develop the watery part of yourself, to
explore the depths of your feelings and to be willing to show your
emotions. He is the only one of the kings to have acknowledged
the feminine side of his nature, his capacity for nurturing, affec-
tion, empathy, and intuition.

His dog is a loyal and loving companion and has lessons to
teach. He is calling on you to show your loyalty and constancy to
some person or objective. Dog calls on you to be friendly and loving. Have you been tactless and unsociable? Are you being too
cynical? Are you being self-righteous at the expense of others? Do
you have the feeling that the whole world is against you and that
everyone has an ulterior motive? Perhaps you have been working
too hard for a good cause and neglecting yourself.

The King of Cups may make his influence felt in your life in the
shape of an actual person. He is a mature man, intensely concerned
with relationships, who often seeks to help others come to terms
with their own emotional problems as a social worker or therapist.
Like many such concerned people, his own personal life is not
without problems. His depth of compassion makes him moody and
sensitive, and he has probably chosen his vocation because a deep
hurt in his own past enables him to empathize with others. He is
the archetypal wounded healer. Because of this, he finds it hard to
trust people and impossible to fully relinquish control. However, he
will always be willing to talk and help you explore your feelings and
come to terms with them. If you need support of a more practical
nature, it might be best to look elsewhere.

Reverse Meanings

The appearance of the King of Cups reversed in your spread indicates that you have too much water in your makeup, a propensity toward overindulgence in sensuality and idleness. The card may indicate alcohol or drug abuse. You may have great enthusiasm for new ideas and projects, but never follow them up, or you dabble in various things without completing any of them. You want spiritual awareness, but are not prepared to work at it, flitting from one idea to another. While this continues, you will make no progress. You may seek to heal others without having first healed your own wounds. This situation can only lead to boredom and melancholy.

The King of Cups reversed may be warning you not to take advice from a well-intentioned but hasty friend. He has your interests at heart but is not reliable.

Suit of Discs

Element: earth

Season: winter
Samhain day to Imbolc Eve

Color: green

Attributes: material things,
the physical plane

Direction: north

Festival: the midwinter solstice
Yule

Ace of Discs

The card shows a highly polished golden disc surrounded by mistletoe. It appears over Drombeg Stone Circle in Ireland.

The Symbolism

The Ace of Discs is the root of the powers of Earth. It is the magical tool of the north and appears in various guises as the shield, the pentacle, the mirror, and the stone of Fal. In Celtic myth, the Lia Fal is the stone of destiny, truth, and wisdom, which the Tuatha de Dannan brought from the Otherworld city of Falias (*truth*).

The suit of discs corresponds to the element of earth, the season of winter, midnight, and the direction of the North. Its station on the wheel is the midwinter solstice, which we call Yule, when the sun is reborn at the dead time of the year when the earth sleeps. From this point on, the days begin to lengthen once more and, though the worst of the winter weather is still to come, we have the promise of the return of spring.

Magically, the earth rules the body and the material plane, including such things as money and possessions. Earth is solid, the manifest world that supports and nourishes us. It is the standing stone beneath the stars, the silent cave, the sacred grove, the high mountain peak, the fertile fields, the crystals, rocks, and stones—our home planet. It is the power of touch and all that is solid and tangible.

The disc is shown over Drombeg Stone Circle, also known as the Druid's Altar, which is located in County Cork in Ireland. The circle is thirty-one feet in diameter and consists of seventeen honey-colored smooth sandstone pillars. It is aligned to the winter solstice sunset, which can be observed from the recumbent stone, set in a notch in the hillside a mile away. For generations, the people of Drombeg visited the circle at the midwinter solstice to solicit the return of the sun and the summer.

The disc of this card is decorated with one of the most important power plants of the midwinter solstice, the mistletoe. This was a sacred herb of the Druids, known as *druad-lus* meaning "the Druid's plant" because it does not grow from the earth but from a "place between places." It is especially sacred when found on the oak, but rarely grows there. At midwinter the berries take on a golden tint and become the "golden bough." Around the midwinter solstice, a druid would cut the mistletoe with a golden sickle. The mistletoe would be caught on a white cloth before it could touch the earth, which was believed to ground its power. The mistletoe would then be distributed to the population at large as a cure-all.

Among the Celts, all warfare had to cease at the time of the cutting of the mistletoe, thus the season of the solstice became a time of peace and goodwill long before Christianity. The mistletoe berries, representing semen as they did, were considered a fertility charm. We still kiss under the mistletoe at Christmas, although traditionally a berry should be removed for each kiss.

Divinatory Meanings

The Ace of Discs represents the root of the powers of earth. The surge of raw energy it engenders enables something to be made manifest in the physical world. It heralds a renewal of ambitions directed toward material creation and financial success.

The appearance of the Ace of Discs in your spread indicates the beginning of an enterprise that will bring financial rewards. Money becomes available to get your projects off the ground— perhaps through legacies, grants, or investments. You now have the energy and resolve to make things work.

This card does not only relate to business and financial matters, but also taking the creative inspiration of the Ace of Wands and turning it into physical works of art, whether paintings, sculptures, books, or music.

However, the energy of the Ace of Discs can blind you to other possibilities in life, you may be susceptible to an unhealthy love of money and the desire to own beautiful things—including people—with no regard for any underlying truth or spirit they may contain. You may initiate relationships that are purely sexual.

Reverse Meanings

The Ace of Discs reversed indicates that you have closed your eyes to everything that goes beyond the material. Your pleasures are derived purely from the physical realm, whether they be eating, drinking, having sex, or buying things. You have become rather greedy and want more and more, but remain dissatisfied. You are blocking out whole realms of possibilities for personal fulfillment. Do you remember the person you used to be—full of dreams and potentials? It is time to get back in touch with this side of yourself again and become a human being, not just a consumer.

Two of Discs

The card shows two discs decorated with basil leaves, moving in harmony and balance with each other. In the background are the Grey Ladies circle and Robin Hood's Walk in Derbyshire, England.

The Symbolism

The two discs move backward and forward: first one is higher, then the other. They are in constant motion.

They are decorated with basil leaves. In medieval England, there was controversy about the powers of basil. Some believed it was poisonous. Culpepper reported a case where a man smelled basil so often that a scorpion grew in his brain, while others considered it good for cheering the spirit and clearing the brain. Magically, basil is an herb of the seeming opposites of death and immortality.

The Grey Ladies or Nine Stones lie on Harthill Moor in Derbyshire, England. In fact, there are only four stones left now, though in the mid-nineteenth century, six were recorded and there may once have been nine. However, nine in the title of a circle often bears no relationship to the number of stones it actually contains. Scholars have invented tortuous explanations relating *nine* to *noon*, saying that many stones are said to come alive and dance at midday. In fact, few stones are meant to come alive at midday; most reserve this power for certain times of the year or midnight, which is the time the Grey Ladies are said to come alive and dance.

Robin Hood's Stride, a natural rocky outcrop on the hillside, is near the Grey Ladies. The two stone pillars, or *tors*, are known as the Weasel and the Inaccessible and are marked with Bronze Age cup and ring marks. They probably played a significant part in Pagan worship as they are surrounded by a number of prehistoric sites, including several circles, barrows, and caves. The Robin Hood of the title is the Green Man, the vital and fecund spirit of earth energy. According to local legend, the Grey Ladies were seven maidens who were turned to stone when they saw Robin Hood urinating from the top of the tors. There are several local associations with Robin Hood, since Little John is said to have been born in the village of Hathersage, which lies a few miles away, and place names such as Hood Brook, Little John's Well, Robin Hood's Cross, and Robin Hood's Cave are all nearby. Little John's bow, which was six feet seven inches long, is said to have been kept in the local church until the nineteenth century, while a ten-foot grave in the churchyard is reputedly his resting place.

Divinatory Meanings

Here the power of the Ace is polarized and its energy must be given direction and made manifest.

Fluctuations in your fortune make projects difficult, and you will need to be flexible in your approach. The Two of Discs shows that there will be changes, but where there are losses there will also be gains. If you put in the hard work, you will be rewarded. Your finances will need careful handling and you must budget carefully and avoid purchasing on credit.

This card indicates visits to friends, but you should be aware that if you have begun a recent love affair, they do not approve of your choice of partner.

Spiritually, the Two of Discs calls on you to learn to move with the ebb and flow of energies, the cycles of being, the tides of life—things need to change to live; stagnation is death.

Reverse Meanings

The Two of Discs reversed indicates that you seem to be unable to finish anything you start or perhaps even keep a job. You are more concerned with the pleasures of the moment and are spending money you cannot afford. If you are not careful you will find yourself in debt.

Dedication

3 of Discs

Three of Discs

The card shows three intricately carved discs. In the background is Chysauster Village in Cornwall.

The Symbolism

The three discs of the card are beautifully carved with images from the Gunderstrup cauldron, obviously by a master craftsman. The Gunderstrup cauldron is one of the best known and most impressive of Celtic artifacts. It is a ritual object made of silver and has several illustrations, including one of a stag-horned Cernunnos surrounded by animals, sitting cross-legged and holding a ram-headed serpent in his left hand. On his right is a stag. He is the Lord of the Underworld, the keeper of the treasures of the earth, its metals and precious stones, and its mysteries of regeneration. An internal panel depicts a parade of warriors being plunged into a cauldron in a ceremony of rebirth.

The discs are shown in the foreground of Chysauster prehistoric village, located near Penzance in Cornwall. There are several houses, each with a central courtyard complete with hearths and drainage systems, gardens, workrooms, and cattle sheds. Farming was executed with terraced fields on the nearby hillside. It was occupied until well into the Roman times. There is also a ruined *fogou* on the site.

A fogou is a manmade tunnel with in inward-curving roof made from roughly shaped granite blocks, some of which extend to sixty-feet long. They were probably constructed in the early Iron Age. In Britain, they appear to be a purely Cornish phenomena, usually in areas associated with mining in prehistoric times. Collecting metal ore and crystals from the womb of the earth was a magical process, fraught with danger and requiring reparation and gratitude toward the Underworld beings. In a time when most houses were made of timber and thatch, the permanence of the materials used and the amount of labor involved indicates that the fogous were important structures. The stone passageway covered by a mound is reminiscent of the earlier burial barrows. There is a single entrance, smaller than the tunnel itself, which would mean that anyone had to crouch down to get in. They are usually oriented facing the midsummer sunrise and the midwinter sunset. The fogou is an earth womb, fertilized by the power of the sun. It is a place for healing, ritual, and regeneration.

Divinatory Meanings

The Three of Discs is the card of the craftsman, including the writer and artist. In an age of mass production, these skills are not as honored as they once were, when they were tinged with a magical mystique. The craftsman's abilities are hard won: natural inclinations and abilities have to be trained, honed, and refined. Imagine the difficulties that faced the creator of the Gunderstrup cauldron, who had no modern tools and machinery to aid him, yet he still managed to produce one of the most beautiful artifacts we know. This card speaks of the dedication and pure hard work necessary to be a craftsman. If you are prepared to expend this tremendous effort, you will gain the admiration and acclaim of your peers—you certainly have the raw talent, but your skills need to be trained and developed. It may be that you are about to embark on a course of study. As with all the threes, this card marks the completion of the first part of a life journey, and you are entitled to congratulate yourself for what you have achieved so far, but bear in mind that there is more to come, and you should approach the future with resolution and careful consideration.

Spiritually, this card shows that you have made a certain amount of progress through natural ability. To go any further, you must apply some disciplined methods of working and commit yourself to following them. It may be that you need to find a teacher or a group of like-minded people to help you.

Reverse Meanings

The Three of Discs reversed shows that you have become preoccupied with money and possessions, and rather than making them work for you or using them to help others, you are only interested in hoarding them in the fashion of a miser. You are missing out on a lot of opportunities in life because you fear losing what you have—mere things that, after all, bring you little real pleasure or benefit. It is time to take an honest look at your life and to decide what is really important.

Four of Discs

The card shows four jeweled discs arranged in a diamond pattern.

The Symbolism

The four discs of this card are highly polished and studded with precious stones. They glitter and sparkle, blinding the eye to the beautiful landscape that lies behind them, which is lush and full of promise, but totally ignored.

Divinatory Meanings

You are assigning far too much importance to possessions. Material acquisitiveness is dominating your life. It is often said that money is the root of all evil, but the actual quote is "greed is the root of all evil." Money is only metal and paper, it is your attitude toward it that is in question. A person who clings too tightly to their money and material possession, and values themselves in terms of what they own, is betraying a lack of personal worth. The point of money is that it circulates, it is redeemed against goods and skills. Anyone who clings to it is demonstrating blocks of various kinds—including blocked energy, creative blocks, and blocked self-expression—which result in internal and external stagnation. You are only interested in the material world and possessions, you can see nothing beyond. You need to be able to let go of things you no longer need, including emotions, in order to move forward and let your energies and creativity flow freely.

Spiritually this is a barren card, you can see nothing beyond the material.

Reverse Meanings

The Four of Discs reversed in your spread indicates that you are suspicious of others. You fear delegating authority because you do not wish to lose total control over your circumstances, business, or possessions to another. You greedily want to hold all the cards. However, this is preventing you from moving forward and achieving more than you already have.

Restriction

5 of Discs

Five of Discs

The card shows five rusty shields bound up with blackthorn. In the background are the Rollright Stones.

The Symbolism

The Rollright Stones are said to be the remains of a king and his men. The army had conquered Britain up to the point of the village of Little Rollright but were prevented from going any further by a witch, who tricked them and turned them to stone.

Perhaps the five rusty, neglected shields of this card once belonged to them. They are shown bound and restricted by blackthorn, *straif* in ogham, which translates as *strife*. The words *slay* and *sloe*, the berries of the blackthorn, are also closely linked.

The blackthorn has an ominous image. The thorns of the blackthorn were used for pricking wax images for cursing. When witches were burned, blackthorn sticks were thrown onto the fire. The *shillelagh*, or Irish club, is made from the dense, heavy blackthorn. In some magical traditions, the blackthorn is the tree of cursing or is used to summon The Wild Hunt. However, blackthorn in ogham sayings is "the increaser of secrets" and "the rune of the great wheel," demonstrating its importance.

It is a tree of great density and strength: the wood is used for weapons and protective clubs. Any weapon or staff made from blackthorn must be used with great care, for strength and power without compassion and wisdom can just as easily destroy the wielder as the target. The energy of the sloe is a difficult one to assimilate and can trap the unwary.

Divinatory Meanings

The Five of Discs indicates that your life becomes bound by enforced restrictions. The likely cause of this is financial difficulty. You may have lost your job or business, or just not have enough money to make ends meet and have to rely on your family and friends to help you. If you think that possessions equal worth, you will undergo a crisis of personal confidence. However, perhaps you should consider this as an opportunity to reconsider your attitudes and develop a sense of self-worth based on who you are, rather than what you do or what you own. No one can take this kind of confidence away from you, and with it you will be well equipped to move forward into a more fulfilling future.

Depending on the surrounding cards, the Five of Discs can also indicate disappointment in love. You feel as though no one understands or cares about you. Do not become overly emotional and try to view the situation clearly. Have faith in yourself and try to see the situation as a challenge from which you can make a new and better start.

Spiritually, this card indicates isolation and loneliness. For the time being, it is probably better for you to work alone. You need to explore your motives and gain a better understanding of your inner self before moving on.

Reverse Meanings

The Five of Discs appearing reversed in your spread shows that you find yourself in financial difficulties, perhaps due to long-term unemployment. If so, it may be time to reconsider your career goals and retrain for a new profession. However, the situation may only be temporary and this should be indicated by surrounding cards.

Six of Discs

The card shows six finely polished discs. In the background is Bol-lowall Barrow, over which a waxing moon rises. Centaury flowers appear at the edge of the picture.

The Symbolism

The six beautiful, rainbow-colored discs of this card appear against the background of Bollowall Barrow in Cornwall, which looks out over the sea toward the Isles of Scilly. It was built using the dry stone method; there is an outer wall with two concentric inner walls. These may have had a ritual function, separating the various stages of death and rebirth. The entrance chamber is oriented to the new moon of winter and the midsummer sun is visible rising over Carn Kenidjack.

As the moon waxes and wanes, she pulls with her the tides of the sea and the tides of life; she influences all that is living. The Wise Women who worked with the power of herbs understood this energy. As the moon waxes, the energy flows upward into the leaves and stalks of the plants. As she wanes the virtue travels to the roots. Thus the bounty of the earth, sun, and moon combines to provide us with herbs for healing and plants for food.

Centaury has always had a great reputation as a healing herb and is the patron plant of herbalists. The Old English name of Fel-wort meant something like "bitter plant" and it was used in the treatment of snakebites and fevers. In the medieval period, centaury was associated with witches, who were said to use it to achieve trance states. For those studying herb craft, centaury is taken as a tea to gain initial communion with the plant spirits in general. It is used as a dedicatory drink for the herbalist, a mark of intention toward the herb kingdom.

Divinatory Meanings

The Six of Discs indicates that you will be the beneficiary of some-one else's bounty. Perhaps you will receive a grant, an award or a monetary gift, or just some good advice. This will put your financial affairs on a firmer footing and restore your waning faith in yourself. This card calls on you to remember that you have been helped by the generosity of another, and that in turn you should be generous with your own time and advice when someone needs it.

Depending on the surrounding cards, the Six of Discs can be warning you not to rush into a love affair or a hasty marriage because the relationship will not last.

This is the card of the herbalist. Herbs are the natural healers provided by the bounty of the Goddess and their powers resonate on a number of levels—physical, mental, and spiritual. Perhaps you are interested in studying the craft of herbs or would benefit from consulting an herbalist.

Reverse Meanings

The Six of Discs reversed indicates that you have lost something because you were negligent; it may have been stolen from you. This reversed card is warning you to be more careful, not to waste things and throw money away.

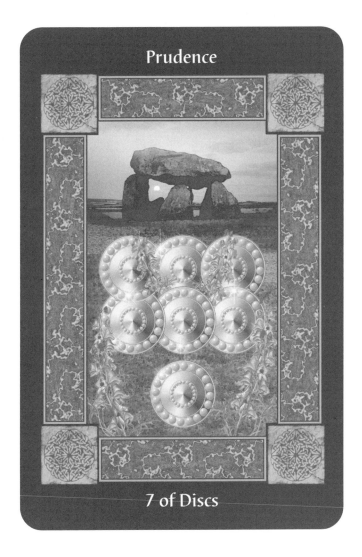

Seven of Discs

Six discs are laid out in a pattern, while one disc, which cannot fit into the existing structure, remains. Monkshood grows in the corner of the card, and in the background is the Carreg Samson cromlech.

The Symbolism

The seven discs of this card are a rich gold. They appear bright and attractive and much more alluring than the dark background of a winter evening. Six of the discs form an overlapping block, while the seventh remains outside the structure of the others.

In the background of this card is the Carreg Samson cromlech or quoit, a Neolithic burial chamber in Wales. It consists of seven upright stones, three of which support the capstone. The whole structure would once have been covered by earth.

In the corner of the card is a monkshood or aconite plant, in earlier times a popular and deadly poison. It was a traditional ingredient of the "flying ointment," though this is as likely to kill you as take you flying—the dose needed to achieve the hallucinogenic effect falls within the lethal limit. Aconite has many connections with the Underworld and death for obvious reasons. It has a dark and fearful reputation and has nearly always been used for malevolent magic.

Divinatory Meanings

The Seven of Discs indicates that you are not prepared to work for what you want, but think you can take a shortcut. A get-rich-quick scheme that seems too good to be true is too good to be true. Invest in it and you will lose a considerable amount of money. If you are hoping that a big gambling win will change your life, you are in for a disappointment. These pipe dreams are preventing you from putting in the time and consistent effort you really need to be successful. You may be neglecting a profitable occupation in favor of mirages that will provoke quarrels and earn you criticism.

Spiritually, this card is warning you that there are no shortcuts to growth and that you should beware of any person or any sect that offers them. You cannot buy it or take it in a pill—you must earn it.

Reverse Meanings

The Seven of Discs reversed indicates that you encounter financial problems and possible bankruptcy due to bad investments or gambling. You are warned to be more prudent in the future!

Eight of Discs

This card shows seven carved discs; one more disc is unfinished.
The background is a winter landscape in Kerry.

The Symbolism

Seven of the stone discs in this card are skillfully carved with the double spiral motif, which represents the life journey. One more disc remains as yet untouched. The background is a winter landscape, late in the year. It is one of those rare days when the air is clear and the sun paints the earth with beautiful, mature colors.

Divinatory Meanings

The Eight of Discs indicates initiating various changes later in life than is thought usual. This is often the card that represents a mid-life crisis, but at any age you might decide that a different career or lifestyle would be more rewarding. Putting such ideas into practice can be quite frightening, as you risk losing what you have already achieved, but a new energy and greater satisfaction can come from it. It may be that you decide to change your career, either developing a hobby or a new interest into a job, or retraining and learning new skills. This is a particularly fortuitous card for the artist who decides to dedicate himself or herself to an artistic career in maturity.

Depending on the surrounding cards, the Eight of Discs can indicate a marriage late in life or a new phase in an existing relationship. This can be a travel card, particularly concerning a honeymoon or second honeymoon.

Reverse Meanings

Financially, you should take note of the old saying "penny wise but pound foolish": it is no good trying to economize on small things while still spending large amounts of money on bigger ones. This card is advising you to plan your financial strategy carefully. At the moment you are unlikely to have more than small sums of money coming in, and it is wise to save what you can.

Spiritually, this reversed card is telling you that you have a tendency to get bogged down in the minutiae of knowledge, categorizing and cataloging various systems. Stop looking at your feet and turn your gaze to the stars, open your heart and allow your spirit to experience the awe and beauty of the cosmos.

Nine of Discs

The card shows nine steel discs depicted against the background of a windswept crag and a stormy sky.

The Symbolism

The nine steel discs of this card, representing material affairs, are highly polished and well maintained. They overlap and are arranged in a stable formation.

However, the background depicts a windblown crag against a dark sky. Though the earth—material element—is stable, the air—mind element—is stormy.

Divinatory Meanings

The Nine of Discs indicates considerable financial gain. This may be the result of your past prudence, thrift, and hard work: a reward for your efforts and careful administration. This is also the card of unearned money received from unexpected sources such as inherited wealth, winnings, gifts, settlements, or alimony. In either case, good luck attends your material affairs.

However, this does not bring you the satisfaction you thought it would. You feel restless and would like a new challenge; you would like to change your life, to travel and have adventures. Your present relationship is also a source of discontent and you are tempted to embark on a new one. Spiritually, you feel that you are not developing. You should avoid making any hasty decisions and consider your future carefully.

Reverse Meanings

The Nine of Discs reversed indicates financial gain from tainted sources or money obtained by theft or embezzlement. Either you are fully aware of the source of this money, or you suspect—it is a matter for your own conscience whether you accept it. Just remember that ultimately there is a price to be paid for everything.

Ten of Discs

The card shows ten discs arranged in a triangle. They are located in a steep valley and rooks circle in the dark sky.

The Symbolism

The ten polished discs of this card are arranged in a stable trian-gular structure, reminiscent of some family crest or heraldic device. They are located on the floor of a steep-sided valley that would be difficult to climb out of. Three rooks fly across the dark and somber sky.

Rooks are birds of omen and are thought to be able to predict the future; they know when the tree in which they are nesting is about to fall and will move out. According to superstition, if rooks leave their accustomed settlement it means bad luck for the landowner, for he will not have an heir. If they build high, the summer will be fine; if low, the weather will be wet and cold. If they perch together, facing the wind, a storm is on the way. The wet and windy weather of early winter is said to make them go crazy, soaring high and making display flights.

Many magicians have noticed that rooks will gather around a cast circle at the power time of dusk, as though they wish to observe and participate in the ritual. They are considered to be wise birds who collect together in a "parliament" to discuss mat-ters. Though it is lucky if they nest on your land, they are sacred to Death Goddesses, such as the Morrigan, Badb, and Macha as they are wont to feed on the corpses of slain warriors.

Divinatory Meanings

This card is concerned with family and tradition. It may concern family wealth, property, or an heirloom passed on—material security based on the work of others in the past. Perhaps you are impelled to research your family history and bloodline or found a dynasty of your own. Perhaps a family home is about to be bought or sold.

On another level, this card may concern the creation of some-thing that can be passed down to future generations, whether it be setting up a business; building or restoring property; or a creating a painting, poem, or piece of music.

Spiritually, the Ten of Discs is advising you that progress will come from traditions founded in the far past, ancestral knowledge and spiritual contact with the ancestors gained in meditations and vision quests.

Reverse Meanings

The Ten of Discs reversed is warning you that you have become stuck in a rut without realizing it. Wake up and seek new challenges! Exercise your intellect and your imagination before it is too late and create something you would be proud to leave to posterity, whether it is a beautiful family, a business, or a creative achievement.

Spiritually, you are just going through the motions, the outward forms. You seem to have stopped looking for a meaning to your life and questing for your personal truth. There is no point in going through the cozy, familiar routines of a religion if your heart and spirit are not involved. You may need help from a spiritual advisor to re-awaken your dormant spiritual life.

This reversed card can also point to problems with wills and trusts, and disagreements about money in the family.

Health

Page of Discs

Page of Discs

The card shows a young man dressed in green. He kneels in a winter clearing with his shield beside him. Late dandelions appear in the foreground.

The Symbolism

The Page of Discs is depicted as a vital young man clad in a green tunic and cloak. He rests briefly in a leafless clearing before resuming his duties. His pose indicates that he is ready to take up his shield and spring into action. He seems to be enjoying the brisk winter air.

At his feet grow some late dandelions, flowers very much associated with solar powers. Its golden color and nourishing vitamin and mineral content make the dandelion a plant of bright energy and vitality. The white, downy seeds also associate it with lunar energies, supplying the balancing spirit. For magic, the seeds are collected under the light of the full moon

Divinatory Meanings

The Page of Discs is the card of health. Awareness of the body is the first impulse of the element of earth. Pay attention to the needs of your physical body and your health. You need to eat a better diet and balance exercise and relaxation in equal measure. If you are in a stressful situation this becomes all the more important; neglect yourself and you will become ill. It is important to recognize the interconnection between mind, body, and spirit and take a holistic approach.

The influence of the Page may be felt in your life in the shape of a real person, a young man or woman. The Page is a perfectionist—fastidious, neat and tidy. He has a sharp, analytical mind but he can be harshly critical. He dislikes waste, idleness, and crowds, and hates displays of sentimentality. The Page has a practical nature, is disciplined, hard-working, and is selflessly devoted to his friends and family. If you should become ill, he would be willing to nurse you carefully, but don't expect sympathy. He is concerned with his own health and diet and may be a member of one of the medical or caring professions. Though he is capable of a steadfast and loyal love, the Page is rather aloof—unemotional and completely unromantic. Left to his own devices he is probably quite happy to be celibate. He does not really need other people; he is a self-contained loner.

Reverse Meanings

A selfish and greedy person, probably a relative, will cause you problems. This person is very critical, fussy, and overly meticulous in small details. They are obsessed with their own health and may insist on strict and faddish diets.

This reversed card can indicate the onset of an illness that can be prevented or at least ameliorated by proper care and attention. Do not ignore any early warning symptoms.

Husbandry

Knight of Discs

Knight of Discs

The card shows a stocky young knight with dark brown hair and eyes. He wears a russet tunic over green hose, and a cloak of the same Lincoln green is thrown back over his shoulders. He holds a round shield in his left hand and a drawn sword in his right. The background shows a winter-ploughed field edged with holly bushes.

The Symbolism

It is winter, and the campaigning season is at an end. All the knights and soldiers have returned to their farms to plough their fields and tend their animals. This card shows the Knight of Discs practicing his warrior skills to keep them keen and sharp.

The Knight stands near a holly tree, one of the few plants that remains lush and green throughout the winter. The Green Knight in the story of Gawain was a Holly Knight carrying a holly club. Their contest is the bi-annual fight of the Oak King and the Holly King—Summer and Winter—for the hand of the Goddess Creiddylad. Gawain chops off the Green Knight's head at the Yule festival, and the still-living Green Knight demands that he should be allowed to return the favor.

Holly was a decoration at the Roman Saturnalia, a winter solstice festival during which an ass was sacrificed, killed with holly. The Romans would send fresh holly boughs as a greeting to friends at the Saturnalia. The custom of holly decoration was carried on into the Christian era, although it was not to be brought in until Christmas Eve or allowed to remain after Twelfth Night.

The holly's place in the ogham alphabet is *tinne*, meaning *fire*. From it we get the word *tinder*. It is a dense, stable wood that contains little water and hence will burn when freshly felled. Magically, it is a masculine tree of warrior magic and spiritual strength.

Divinatory Meanings

The Knight of Discs has no grand, world-shaking scheme, but will put his whole effort into achieving what he has set out to do. He is completely steady, reliable, and hardworking. His power is that of the holly. Holly calls upon the seeker to recognize inner strengths, to dispense with petty jealousies and frustrations, and to learn the value of personal sacrifice. Holly was used in making spear shafts, giving them strength and potent life force. Used correctly and with knowledge, this spear becomes one with its user in perfect balance.

The Knight's lesson is that of steady and consistent effort directed to both the small and large tasks in life. He is telling you to develop your practical skills and to learn to rely on yourself rather than on other people. There is much pleasure to be derived from the simple things in life. Satisfaction can be gained from seeing small jobs through to the best of your ability, which is just as well, as you will need to work hard and attend to details to see a matter through. At the moment you will need to be patient and approach people and situations with gentleness.

At this time, you will gain inner peace from contact with the earth and by attending to practical things, perhaps tending your house and garden. Physical labor and exercise will help to relieve stress and enable you to see things in proportion.

The influence of the Knight of Discs may appear in your life in the shape of a young man who will set for you an example of the virtues of hard work, patience, and gentleness. He is a steady, tranquil man who is capable of taking anything in his stride and dealing with it without wasting energy on worry or regret. He has great self-control and strength of character; he acts with a quiet deliberation, patiently working his way through any task or challenge without complaint. He loves the land and the countryside and is happiest in familiar surroundings. As a friend or a lover he is faithful and dependable. He is, however, rather intolerant of impractical people. Though it takes a lot to make him lose his temper, once it is roused it is not easily quenched.

Reverse Meanings

The Knight of Discs reversed is telling you that you have become idle and complacent. You seem to be caught in a spiral of ever-increasing inertia when you feel less and less like doing anything at all. In this case, your solution is not an intellectual resolution, but lies in undertaking physical, practical work. This will help you forget your problems, build up your strength and endurance, burn toxins from your body, and relieve stress so that you can go to bed at the end of the day tired and with a sense of achievement. After a few weeks of this, your energy levels will have increased and you will feel ready to tackle anything.

Expression

Queen of Discs

Queen of Discs

This card shows a woman dressed in green and seated on a golden throne. Her left arm rests on a golden disc. The background is a winter landscape in Kerry, Ireland.

The Symbolism

The card portrays a beautiful black-haired, sloe-eyed woman. Her bright green dress clings to her voluptuous body. She reclines sensuously on a golden throne, confident in herself and her attractiveness. She stares boldly at the observer, her gaze challenging and perhaps exciting. She is like the ivy that grows around her throne, alive and vital whatever the season.

Divinatory Meanings

When the Queen of Discs appears in your spread, she is advising you of the importance of taking pleasure in your own body.

Your body is a sacred gift, given to you to explore the full range of experiences of the physical plane, not to be ignored, denigrated, or abused. You are unique and special. Beauty is not a matter of fitting whatever cultural stereotype is popular at the moment, but is a quality that shines from within.

We live in the material world, interacting with it and with other people; this is natural and good. We are driven to overcome the separateness of the ego or "little self" by having relationships with others. Physical contact nourishes the psyche and is important for physical, mental, and spiritual health. Do not be afraid to touch and hug your partner, your children, or your friends.

Sex with someone you love is one of the deepest forms of communion, the relinquishing of two egos to achieve physical and spiritual unity. This type of true relationship is very rare and precious and one to which most people aspire. It takes time, patience, love, and understanding to develop. Once achieved it should be nurtured, not endangered for the sake of mere mundane sexual flirtations.

The desire for sexual union is one of the basic manifestations of the life force. Only very advanced spiritual beings are able to redirect this energy into the raising of the serpent force within.

The appearance of the Queen of Discs in your spread may indicate that a woman will become important in your life. She is strong and independent, practical, and very fond of good food, clothes, possessions, and pleasure. The Queen is ambitious, she admires success and social position and covets them for herself. Security is important to her; she has her feet firmly on the ground and acts responsibly and with much practical wisdom. She can be a good friend when it suits her, but she is capable of using others for her own ends.

Reverse Meanings

If you have low levels of physical energy and a reduced sexual drive, the life force is not flowing freely within you. If you are avoiding this type of close relationship with another and denying its importance, you should look at the reasons you are depriving yourself of the sharing of love, nourishment, and pleasure. It may be that you are afraid of giving yourself or are afraid of your own sexual power. This also applies to those who have numerous sexual partners, never making a commitment or allowing themselves to become too close to one other person. You should explore your own sensuality and work on clearing the root and sacral chakras.

The Queen of Discs reversed may also be telling you to beware of a woman who uses sex to gain power over others. She is a vain creature whose sense of self-worth is only reflected in the eyes of those who desire or admire her. She needs to constantly boost her ego by new conquests and will not be loyal or reliable as either a friend or a lover.

King of Discs

The card portrays the Lord of the Powers of Earth as a middle-aged man wearing a rich green costume and cloak. He sits upright and alert on a rocky throne, the arms of which are carved into the likeness of boar heads. A robin perches beside him. He wears a crown of holly leaves and berries and holds an iron disc in his hand. The midwinter sun sets in the background.

The Symbolism

In this card, the King of Discs represents the Lord of the Powers of Earth, magically associated with the material plane, touch, expression, wealth, and manifestation. Earth is all that is solid and tangible, from the bones of your body to the rocky bones of the land, from the standing stone to the mountain peak, from the sacred grove to the fertile field, from the tiniest crystal to our home planet. Earth is symbolized by the disc, the pentacle, the mirror, and the shield. Magically, it corresponds to the hour of midnight and the season of winter.

The King of Discs can be seen as the Holly King, ruler of the waning half of the year. He sits at the northern station of the wheel that relates to the day of the winter solstice, the shortest day of the year when the powers of the dark are in ascendance, the day of chaos, the crack between the worlds before the sun is reborn on the next morning.

Among the ancient peoples, the winter was the time of dark, cold, and death, when the darker forces were in ascendance. The holly is evergreen and lasts throughout the winter, representing continuing life, though it is thorny and difficult. It is particularly a tree of the winter solstice, the bright red berries representing the blood and sacrifice of the god, his life and spirit continuing with the evergreens throughout the dark time.

The arms of the King's throne are carved with boar heads, the power animal of the midwinter solstice. The custom of serving a boar's head, with an apple in its mouth and evergreen decorations, was still traditional at Yuletide in medieval times. Folklore festivals also echo the connection of midwinter and the boar's head, a symbol of the fertility of the earth. The last sheaf of the harvest was often called the "sow" and was saved and baked into a loaf in the shape of a boar at midwinter, which was placed on the festive table until the end of the Yuletide season. It was then put away and kept until the spring sowing when part was eaten, and part mixed with the corn. As a familiar, Boar teaches the secrets of transformation, the mystery of renewal in the Underworld and rebirth through death.

The Holly King's familiar bird is the robin, which is associated with fire—particularly the fire of the sun at the winter solstice. Its red breast marks it as a fire totem in the midst of winter, like the red berries of the evergreen holly. It is a bird of the dark, waning half of the year, and undergoes a symbolic battle with the wren, familiar of the Oak King, ruler of the waxing year, at the winter solstice.

In Celtic lore, the robin is one of the birds that gave the gift of fire to humankind, bringing a flaming branch from the sun. In doing so, the robin was burned and its Welsh name *bronrhuddyn* means "singed breast." Offerings were placed out for the robin at Yuletide to ensure luck for the coming year.

Divinatory Meanings

In this card, we meet the quintessential powers of earth in the guise of the King of Discs. Earth is the element most closely associated with the physical body and the environment. It is the incarnating principle, investing spirit with a material form. It is a nourishing element that supports life.

The King of Discs appearing in your spread indicates that it is time to deal and act within the material world, to develop the characteristics of the element of earth within yourself. Earth is concerned with being practical and with making something manifest in the world.

Life is a challenge and the test is how you meet it. Challenges and trials make us grow and build strength of character. You need to hone your courage and determination, to be honest with yourself and others. Don't be taken in by people who seem to offer easy answers or try to look for shortcuts. Don't dissemble, go straight to the heart of the matter and tackle it head on.

Meditate on the power of Boar—he is wild and free, master of his own destiny, courageous and daring. His life force is strong.

Bring some of Boar's power into your own life. Your self-confidence grows as you achieve successes.

Depending on the surrounding cards, the appearance of the King of Discs in your spread can indicate an increase of wealth or successful establishment in a profession, especially one concerned with mathematics or accounting.

The influence of the King of Discs may make itself felt in your life in the shape of a mature man. He is steady, methodical, and reliable. He is practical and deliberate and seems to be able to accomplish anything he sets his mind to. He thinks carefully before he acts, and when he does act, he follows the course he has set for himself without deviation. He is loyal and trustworthy and makes a very good friend, but he can be dangerous if crossed.

Reverse Meanings

The King of Discs reversed is warning you that you have too much earth in your makeup. You are rather ponderous and materialistic and in danger of becoming more than a little dull. You need to develop the other elements within yourself in balance: the creativity and energy of fire, the emotional fulfillment of water, and the intellectual power of air. The challenge here is to become a whole and fully rounded person.

The King of Discs reversed may be warning you to beware of falling under the influence of a tyrannical person who believes that his way is the only way. He has a petty mind and seeks to make others conform to his narrow, materialistic ideas. His heavy-handed methods mask the innate weakness of his character. He equates change and any deviation from his slavishly followed views as a precarious loss of his control—a prospect that fills him with fear.

The Llewellyn Tarot

Anna-Marie Ferguson

Over a century ago, a young boy left Wales and journeyed to America, where he started a small press, now known as Llewellyn Publications. Llewellyn George's adventurous spirit and Welsh heritage embodies *The Llewellyn Tarot*, which also celebrates the publisher's enduring legacy.

From the creator of the popular *Legend: The Authurian Tarot* kit, this lavishly illustrated deck offers universal appeal (based on Rider-Waite) with a Welsh twist. A compelling story unfolds starring Rhiannon as The Empress, Bran the Blessed as The Emperor, The Wild Herdsman as The Horned God (the Devil), Gwydion as The Magician, Llew Llaw Gyffes as the Bringer of Light, and other figures from Welsh mythology. Watercolor imagery beckons us forth into a mystic world of ancient forests, sensuous seascapes, and wondrous waterfalls—gorgeous landscapes brimming with mystery, meaning, and magic. Also included is *The Llewellyn Tarot Companion*, which features an introduction to the craft and history of tarot, along with Welsh legends infused in this deck.

0-7387-0299-4, boxed 5 ⅜ x 8 ¼ kit:
78-full-color cards, bag, 228 p. book   **$24.95**

The Shining Tribe Tarot

Rachel Pollack

Mysterious masked dancers . . . sleepers in dream temples . . . dark spirits rising out of canyon walls … Based on tribal and prehistoric art from around the world, and rooted in the wisdom and tradition of the Tarot itself, the *Shining Tribe Tarot* grew from an earlier deck called *Shining Woman* (based on the World card in the traditional Tarot). This deck uses prehistoric images from the very origins of art: the rock paintings and carvings of Africa, Australia, and America, and the cave art of France, Spain, and Siberia.

This deck draws upon 50,000 years of human encounters with the Divine. Through readings and meditation with the ancient images, the cards can help you discover your own path. The kit includes a comprehensive guide to the deck along with Rachel Pollack's own poetry for each card.

- Incorporates symbolism from the Jewish Kabbala, Jungian psychology, and ancient cultures from around the world
- Changes in the Major Arcana include Tradition for the Hierophant, the Hanged Woman instead of the Hanged Man, and Awakening for Judgement
- Suit cards are changed from Wands to Trees, Cups to Rivers, Swords to Birds, and Stones to Pentacles

1-56718-558-4, boxed kit:
Book: 5¼ x 8, 320 pp.
Deck: 78 full-color cards   **$34.95**

To order, call 1–877–NEW WRLD
Prices subject to change without notice

Shapeshifter Tarot

D. J. Conway and Sirona Knight
Illustrated by Lisa Hunt

Like the ancient Celts, you can now practice the shamanic art of shapeshifting and access the knowledge of the eagle, the oak tree or the ocean: wisdom that is inherently yours and resides within your very being. The Shapeshifter Tarot kit is your bridge between humans, animals and nature. The cards in this deck act as merging tools, allowing you to tap into the many different animal energies, together with the elemental qualities of air, fire, water and earth.

The accompanying book gives detailed explanations on how to use the cards, along with their full esoteric meanings, and mythological and magical roots. Exercises in shapeshifting, moving through gateways, doubling out, meditation and guided imagery give you the opportunity to enhance your levels of perception and awareness, allowing you to hone and accentuate your magical understanding and skill.

1-56718-384-0 boxed kit:
Book: 6 x 9, 264 pp.
Deck: 81 full-color cards   **$31.95**

To order, call 1–877-NEW WRLD

Prices subject to change without notice